AQA GCSE

Foundation: Combined Science Trilogy and Entry Level Certificate

T0347351

Workbook

Rob Butler

OXFORD
UNIVERSITY PRESS

Contents

How to use this book

Key words – All the key words you will need for each chapter is in an easy-to-reference box at the start of each spread.

Practice activities Each chapter has a variety of questions, some for Entry Level Certificate and some for Combined Science Trilogy. You can use these to build your confidence and help you progress through the course.

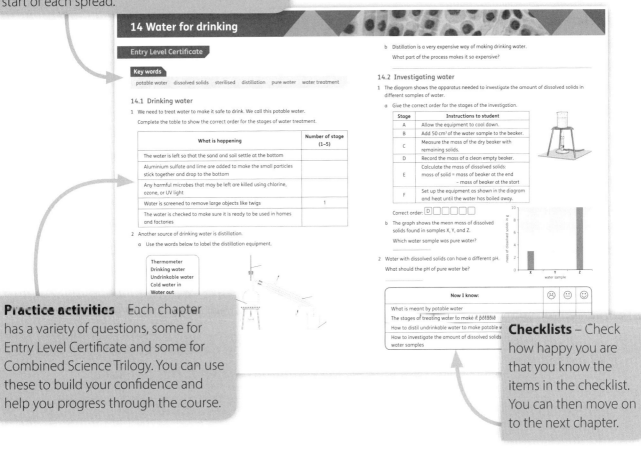

Checklists – Check how happy you are that you know the items in the checklist. You can then move on to the next chapter.

Exam-style questions – These come at the end of each Component to test your knowledge. The answers to these and the practice questions are in the back of the book to help you monitor your progress.

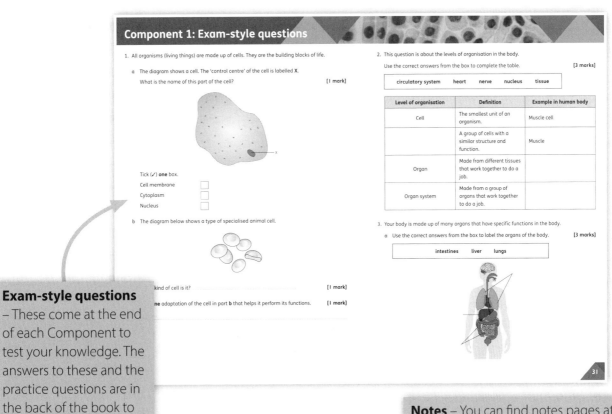

Notes – You can find notes pages at the back of your book for you to write on.

1 What is the body made of?

Key words

cell   cell membrane   cytoplasm   nucleus   tissue   organ   organ systems
heart   circulatory system   artery   vein   blood cells   platelets   enzymes

1.1 Animal cells

1   Cells are made of different parts that have their own jobs to do.

Draw **one** line from each part of the cell to what it does.

Part of the cell	What the part does
Nucleus	The 'filling' of the cell where the chemical reactions happen
Cell membrane	Where the genetic material (DNA) is kept. It controls what the cell does
Cytoplasm	It lets substances pass into and out of the cells

2   Most cells are **specialised**. This means they have a special shape or structure to carry out a particular function.

For each cell type below, describe a special feature that helps with the cell's job.

Cell type	How is it specialised?
Sperm cell head section nucleus tail	
Muscle cell	

1.2 Looking at cells

1 A student used a microscope to look at a slide of some muscle cells.

a Use the correct answers from the box to label the parts of the cell that you can see.

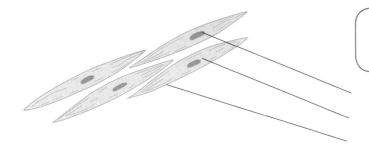

nucleus   cytoplasm
cell membrane

b The magnification of the microscope eyepiece objective was ×10.

The magnification of the objective lens was ×100.

What is the total magnification of the microscope?

_____

1.3 Levels of organisation

1 Cells have to work together in the body to make it function properly.

Put the following levels of organisation in order of increasing size.

Organs   Tissues   Cells   Organ systems

_____   _____   _____   _____

Least complicated ➡ Most complicated

2 Sort the following into tissues, organs, and organ systems.

Liver   Circulatory system   Small intestine   Stomach lining cells
Muscle cells   Stomach   Digestive system   Heart

Tissues	Organs	Organ systems

3 a Name each of these organ systems.

b Write down what the function (job) of each organ system is.

Diagram	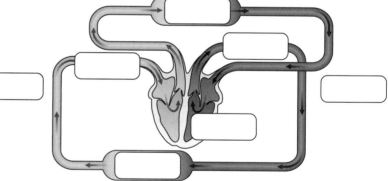		
Name of system			
Function			

1.4 The circulatory system

1 The circulatory system carries blood around the body.

Complete the diagram below by adding the letter of the correct label in each box.

a heart

b lungs

c body organs

d main vein

e oxygenated blood (with lots of oxygen in)

f deoxygenated blood (not much oxygen in)

g main artery

2 What is blood made of? Complete the table.

	Name of component	Diagram	What it does in the blood (its function)
a	Red blood cell		
b			
c			
d		The liquid part of the blood	Liquid (mostly water) that carries blood cells and dissolved substances around the body

1.5 The digestive system

1 The diagram shows the human digestive system.

Use the correct words from the box to label the main parts.

anus   gall bladder
gullet
large intestine
liver   mouth
pancreas
small intestine
stomach

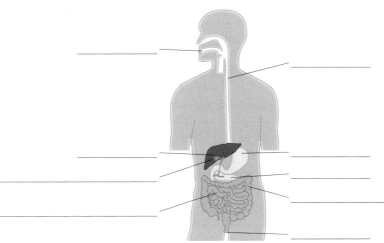

2 This is a flow diagram of digestion in humans.

Write what happens at each stage.

Mouth _____

Stomach _____

Small intestine _____

Large intestine _____

Anus _____

3 Draw **one** line between the organ and the substance it makes.

Then draw **one** line between each substance and what it does.

Organ	Substance	What it does
Mouth	Acid	Contains enzymes. Lubricates food down the oesophagus
Stomach	Saliva	Helps digest proteins and kill bacteria
Liver	Enzymes	Emulsifies fats
Pancreas	Bile	Help break down food in digestion

Now I know:	☹	😐	☺
The main parts of an animal cell			
How some cells are specialised to do a specific job			
How to use a microscope – the parts and how they work			
How to work out the total magnification			
How cells can work together to make tissues, organs, and organ systems			
Where the organs can be found in the body and what they do			
The parts of the human circulatory system and where the blood flows			
The different types of cells found in the circulatory system			
The location and functions of organs that make up the digestive system			

Key words

mitochondria   ribosomes   cell wall   chloroplasts   permanent vacuole   diffusion

osmosis   concentration gradient   capillaries   cardiovascular

carbohydrase   lipase   protease   active site   substrate

1.6 Plant and animal cells

1   The diagram shows an animal cell and a plant cell.

   a   Label each cell and the structures inside them.

_____ cell

_____ cell

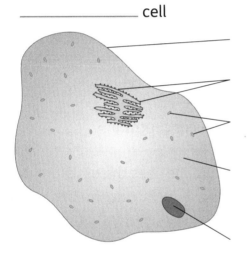

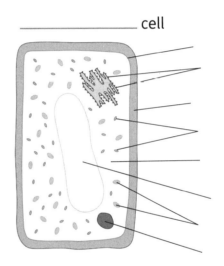

   b   Name **two** things that animal and plant cells have in common.

_____ and _____

   c   Give **two** differences between animal and plant cells.

_____

_____

2 Draw **one** line from each feature of a root hair cell to its function.

Feature	Function
Cell wall	Transfer energy to move minerals into the cell
Mitochondria	Large surface area for absorbing water and minerals
Permanent vacuole	Cellulose structure supports the cell
Root hair	Full of sap, which keeps the cell rigid

1.7 Transport in cells

1 Diffusion is the movement of molecules in a gas or a solution.

Draw an arrow between the two boxes to show which way diffusion occurs.

Low concentration		High concentration

2 A student is shopping in a large shop. Looking across the store, he sees the assistant drop a bottle of perfume and the bottle smashes. A minute later the student can smell the perfume.

The diagram shows how the perfume particles spread out through the air.

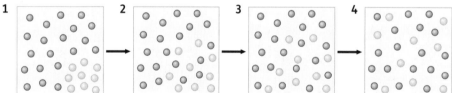

a Explain how the student can smell the perfume when it was dropped at the other side of the shop. These words might help you:

diffuses	low	high	equal	concentration
particles	air	perfume		concentration gradient

The dark particles are the _____

The light particles are the _____

In diagrams 1, when the assistant drops the perfume _____

_____

In diagrams 2 and 3, the particles are _____

_____

In diagram 4, _____

_____

b What is active transport?

_____

_____

1.8 Blood vessels

1 Blood vessels are adapted to their role (job) in the body.

a Draw **one** line from each type of blood vessel to the correct diagram and description of its wall.

Blood vessel	What it looks like	Thickness of the wall
Artery	X	Thick
Vein	Y	One cell thick
Capillary	Z	Thin

b Which vessel carries blood towards the heart? _____

c Which vessel carries blood away from the heart? _____

d Why are the walls of the third type of vessel very thin?

_____

_____

2 The blood vessels that bring oxygen and nutrients to the heart's cells are very important because the heart never stops beating. Sometimes these vessels become blocked.

a   What substance is most likely to build up inside the arteries? _____

b   What happens when the arteries that go to the heart are blocked?

_____

1.9 Enzymes

1   Enzymes are proteins that speed up the rate of a reaction. Some enzymes help digestion.

Complete the table below.

Enzyme	What it breaks down	What is made at the end of the reaction?
Carbohydrases, e.g. amylase		
Lipases		

2   Enzymes are special proteins. They have to be a specific shape to work. This is because the enzyme must be the right shape for the molecule being broken down (the substrate). If it is not the right shape, the enzyme won't work.

a   What happens to the enzyme at the end of the reaction?

_____

b   What happens if the enzyme is denatured (has its shape changed) by getting too hot?

_____

Now I know:	☹	😐	☺
How animal and plant cells are different			
What happens during diffusion in gases and liquids			
What happens in active transport			
How blood vessels in the human body are adapted to their role			
Where the different enzymes are made			
What substrates the enzymes work on			
What happens to the enzyme if it changes shape (is denatured)			

2 How the body works

Key words

respiration   energy   glucose   oxygen   balanced diet   nutrients
carbohydrate   lipid   protein   vitamins and minerals   water
lifestyle   exercise   factors   pulse   rate   beats   fitness   recovery rate

2.1 Respiration

1   In which body organ are the gases exchanged with the atmosphere? _____

2   a   Complete the word equation for aerobic respiration.

    _____ + _____ → _____ + _____ + energy

   b   Name the compounds involved in aerobic respiration that are described in the table.

Description	Name
This gas diffuses into your blood in the lungs. It is carried by red blood cells.	
This gas is carried in the plasma and diffuses out of the blood into your lungs.	
This substance is made by digestion of large food molecules. It is transported in the blood.	

3   Name **two** things that the energy that is transferred during respiration would be used for.

   1   _____

   2   _____

2.2 Healthy diet

1 There are six substances needed as part of a healthy diet.

Draw **one** line from each substance to the foods it is found in, and its use in the body.

Food group	Found in	Use
Carbohydrates	Drinks like juice	Growth and repair
Lipids (fats and oils)	Cereals, fruit, and vegetables	Main source of energy
Proteins	Red meats, butter, and cheese	Store energy and keep you warm
Vitamins and minerals	Starchy food like cereals and potatoes, or sweet food like fruit	Small amounts are needed to help you grow and function normally
Water	Meat, fish, and eggs	Help food move through the gut
Fibre	Fruit and vegetables	Cells and body fluids need this to prevent dehydration

2 Some people have a poor diet.

a If someone eats too much energy-rich food, they can become overweight.

Why is it unhealthy to be overweight?

It is unhealthy to be overweight because _____

_____

b If someone doesn't eat enough energy-containing foods, they may become underweight.

Why is it unhealthy to be underweight?

It is unhealthy to be underweight because _____

_____

2.3 Lifestyle and disease

1 Lifestyle factors can affect your body.

For each factor below, circle whether it has a **positive** or **negative** effect on your health.

Then write **one** effect that each factor has on the body.

a Smoking: **positive / negative** effect

It can _____

b Alcohol: **positive / negative** effect

It can _____

c Exercise: **positive / negative** effect

It can _____

d Eating a lot of energy-rich food: **positive / negative** effect

It can _____

2 Smoking can also be dangerous to people around a smoker.

a What is this risk factor called? _____

b Why is it dangerous?

_____

_____

3 Which of the following health factors is type 2 diabetes often linked to?

Tick **one** box.

being overweight ☐

heavy consumption of alcohol ☐

smoking ☐

2.4 Investigating pulse rate

1 Your resting pulse rate is taken when you are resting, before exercising.

Your recovery time is how long it takes your pulse to return to normal after exercising.

a Describe how you would measure your pulse rate.

_____

_____

b The table shows someone's pulse rate before and after exercise.

Time (mins)	Resting	Exercise	0	1	2	3	4	5	6	7	8
Pulse rate (beats per minute)	75		120	115	110	105	100	92	82	75	75

What is the recovery time for this person? _____ minutes

c Why might you want to measure your pulse rate? (What does your pulse rate tell you?)

_____

_____

Now I know:	☹	😐	☺
The word equation for respiration – reactants and products (chemicals at start and end)			
The main components of a healthy diet			
The purpose of the main nutrient groups in the body			
What happens if our diet isn't balanced			
Some lifestyle factors that have a positive effect on health			
Some lifestyle factors that have a negative effect on health			
What a person's pulse rate might tell you about them			

Key words

| aerobic | anaerobic | energy | lactic acid | ethanol | carbon dioxide |
| risk factors | correlation | positive | negative | relationship | causation |

2.5 Anaerobic respiration

1   Anaerobic respiration happens when there isn't enough oxygen,
for example during intense exercise.

In humans, a chemical is produced when anaerobic respiration takes place.
As it builds up, it can result in muscle pain after even a short period of time.

What is the name of this chemical?

_____

2   Anaerobic respiration can be useful in industry. We call the process fermentation.

a   Give **two** examples of fermentation processes.

Then name the useful product(s) made in each one.

Process 1: _____

Useful product(s): _____

Process 2: _____

Useful product(s): _____

b   How could we test the gas given off in an aerobic respiration, to work out what it is?

_____

_____

2.6 Increasing the risk of disease

1   List **three** risk factors to your health that you are able to control.

1   _____

2   _____

3   _____

2 For each graph in the table below:

– Write the type of correlation shown, if any.

– Describe the link between the factor and the frequency of the disease.

Graph	Type of correlation	What is the link between the factor and disease?
	_____ _____	_____ _____ _____
	_____ _____	_____ _____ _____
	_____ _____	_____ _____ _____

Now I know:	☹	😐	☺
How anaerobic respiration (without oxygen) is different from aerobic respiration (with oxygen)			
Some of the uses of anaerobic respiration			
The products of anaerobic respiration			
Some risk factors that are linked to lifestyle choices			
The different types of correlation between variables			
The difference between correlation and causation			

3 How the body fights disease

Entry Level Certificate

Key words

disease   bacteria   viruses   pathogens   antibodies
vaccination   immune   antibiotics   addiction

3.1 Infectious disease

1 Our bodies have lots of ways of stopping harmful pathogens getting inside our bodies. We call these defence mechanisms.

Draw **one** line from each defence mechanism to how it works.

Defence mechanism   **How it works**

Defence mechanism	How it works
Stomach acid	Trap dirt and pathogens
Hairs and mucus in nose and throat	Ingest pathogens that get inside the body, and produce antibodies
Waterproof skin	Helps break down pathogens
White blood cells	Stops pathogens getting inside the body

2 Pathogens are microorganisms that can make you ill if they get inside your body. The two main types of pathogen are bacteria and viruses.

Put the key words below in the correct boxes to describe the characteristics of bacteria and viruses. Some words may apply to both.

extremely small particles   cause disease   reproduce inside a living cell

treated with antibiotics   produce toxins   microscopic cells   need a host cell

Bacteria	Viruses

3.2 Vaccination

1 Vaccinations are an important tool for stopping the spread of potentially dangerous diseases.

Complete the table below with the correct key terms.

> antibodies immune pathogen white blood cells

Definition	Key term
The part of your body that makes antibodies.	
This makes you ill. It could be a virus or bacteria (or protozoon).	
This is when your body knows how to produce antibodies so you don't get ill from a pathogen.	
These are molecules that attach to a pathogen and help the body destroy it.	

2 How does vaccination work?

The boxes below show the important stages in the vaccination against a pathogen.

Describe what happens at each stage.

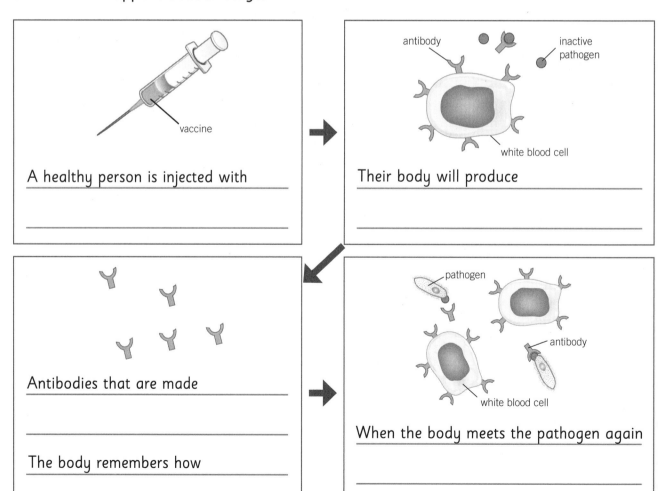

A healthy person is injected with _____

_____

Their body will produce _____

_____

Antibodies that are made _____

_____

The body remembers how _____

_____

When the body meets the pathogen again _____

_____

3.3 Medical drugs

1 Medical drugs are drugs that benefit your health.

One of the main types of drugs used to treat infectious diseases is antibiotics.

a Which of these diseases can be treated with antibiotics?

Tick **one** box.

The flu (caused by a virus) ☐

Syphilis (a bacterial infection) ☐

b How did you choose your answer?

_____

2 Sometimes drugs can have unwanted effects when we take them.

Some drugs are illegal because of the effects they have on the body.

Complete the table below with the correct key terms.

> addiction   side effects   withdrawal symptoms

Definition	Key term
When a drug has effects on the body that are not intended – for example, thalidomide caused birth defects in unborn babies.	
When it is hard to stop taking a drug because your body becomes dependent on it – for example, someone taking an illegal drug like heroin.	
The effects on the body when you stop taking a drug that you are dependent on – for example, stopping smoking.	

3 Penicillin is a drug that has saved millions of lives.

What type of drug is penicillin?

Tick **one** box.

antibiotic ☐

antiseptic ☐

antiviral ☐

hormone ☐

painkiller ☐

3.4 Testing the effect of antibiotics

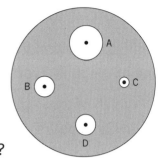

1   An antibiotic stops bacteria growing and reproducing.
    We can test how effective antibiotics are in a laboratory.

    Look at the diagram of a Petri dish and answer the questions.

    a   Which of the antibiotics being tested is most effective, and why?

    The most effective antibiotic is _____ .

    I can tell this because _____

    _____

    b   What do we call the space around the antibiotic where no bacteria grow?

    _____

    c   Name a piece of apparatus in the lab that you could use to
        measure the size of A, B, C, or D.

    _____

2   Which of these chemicals could you use on a kitchen surface to kill bacteria?
    Tick **one** answer.

    Antibiotic   ☐

    Anti-viral drug   ☐

    Disinfectant   ☐

Now I know:	☹	😐	☺
The different types of pathogens (bacteria and viruses)			
How white blood cells help fight infectious diseases			
How the body fights infectious diseases			
How vaccination works to cause immunity to an infectious disease			
Some examples of types of medical drugs and their effects			
What antibiotics do and how to compare their effectiveness in a Petri dish			

bacteria   viruses   multiply   transmission   communicable   clinical trials

3.5 Bacteria and viruses

1   Bacteria and viruses are different in the way they reproduce.

Explain how bacteria and viruses reproduce.

Bacteria	Viruses
Bacteria reproduce by splitting	Viruses reproduce by taking over

2   Bacteria grow very quickly.

A piece of raw chicken has been left out in a warm place for 3 hours.

a   There are 10 bacterial cells present at the start.

Calculate how many bacteria there would be after three hours
if each bacterial cell can divide once every 20 minutes.

There is a quick way to calculate the final bacterial population using this formula:

$$\text{final population} = \text{initial population} \times 2^{\text{number of bacterial divisions}}$$

Time	0 m	20 m	40 m	1 hr	1 hr 20 m	1 hr 40 m	2 hrs	2 hrs 20 m	2 hrs 40 m	3 hrs
Number of bacteria	10									

b   Imagine the same chicken but with 25 bacteria present at the start.

How many will there be after 9 bacterial divisions? _____

3.6 Preventing the spread of disease

1 Pathogens are spread (transmitted) in different ways.

Draw **one** line from each method of spread of pathogens to how it happens and to an example.

Type of spread	What happens	Example
Air	Touching someone who is ill or something that has pathogens on it	Diseases like cholera are caught by drinking dirty water
Direct contact	Disease-causing bacteria that are present in food	Sexually transmitted diseases, or touching contaminated door handles
Food	Untreated water can contain bacteria or viruses from human or animal sewage	On a plane, if one person sneezes droplets containing pathogens into the air, other people will breathe them in and become ill
Water	Breathing in droplets that somebody has sneezed out	Eating raw chicken that might contain *Salmonella* bacteria

2 How do we stop the spread of the following diseases? Complete the table.

Disease	How do we stop the spread?
Colds and influenza	
Food poisoning	
Sexually transmitted diseases	
Malaria (spread through mosquito bites)	
Waterborne diseases like cholera	

3.7 Testing new drugs

1 New drugs have to be tested before they are used with lots of people.

Complete the table to show which statements about drug testing are true or false.

Statement	True or false?
Drugs are tested to make sure they are not addictive.	
Drugs are tested to make sure they work as expected.	
Drugs are tested to make sure they cause side effects.	
Drugs are tested on healthy volunteers as well as those who are ill.	

2 Drugs have to be tested thoroughly before they are used on patients.

Match the labels to the pictures to complete the order that a new drug is tested.

Small-scale tests on people	Laboratory (in vitro) testing	Testing on animals
Small-scale testing with ill people	Drug designed on computer or isolated from nature	Large-scale testing on lots of people

1. _____   2. _____   3. _____

4. _____   5. _____   6. _____

Now I know:	🙁	😐	🙂
The differences between bacteria and viruses			
How bacteria and viruses reproduce and the differences between them			
What is meant by a communicable disease			
Some of the ways infectious diseases are spread			
How the spread of infectious diseases can be prevented			
Useful characteristics of new drugs			
How new drugs are tested			

4 How the body is coordinated

Key words

nervous system	reflex actions	neuron	reaction times	menstrual cycle
period	hormones	contraception		infertility

4.1 Nervous system

1   The nervous system is a control system for our bodies.

A reflex action is a special kind of nervous response that helps to keep the body safe.

Which of these are features of a reflex action? Tick all the correct answers.

A   Very fast ☐

B   Always involves the brain ☐

C   Carried around the body in the blood ☐

D   Carried around the body by nerves ☐

E   Slow ☐

F   Does not involve the brain ☐

2   Tick the situations that are examples of reflex actions.

A   The pupil changing size in bright or dim light ☐

B   Sneezing when you inhale some dust ☐

C   Blood glucose levels dropping after a meal ☐

D   The knee-jerk reaction ☐

E   The hormone adrenalin making your heart beat faster ☐

4.2 Testing reactions

1   A student measured reaction times using a metre ruler by dropping and catching it.
The number on the ruler was converted to a reaction time in seconds by using a table (to look up the reaction time).

The reaction times were compared to those of a friend to see who had the fastest reaction time.

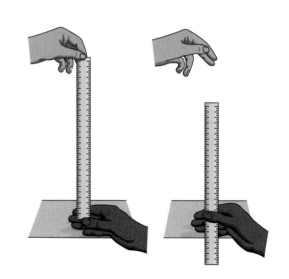

A student carried out this experiment and collected the results below.

	Attempt 1	Attempt 2	Attempt 3	Mean
Student	0.2 s	0.3 s	0.2 s	_____ s
Friend 1	0.2 s	0.3 s	0.4 s	_____ s
Friend 2	0.4 s	0.3 s	0.3 s	_____ s

a   Calculate the mean for each person (to two decimal places) and write it in the table.

b   Which person had the fastest reaction time? _____

c   What is the advantage of repeating the experiment three times rather than just doing
it once?

_____

_____

2   Name **one** factor that might speed up your reaction time. _____

3   Name **one** factor that might slow down your reaction time. _____

4.3 Hormones and the menstrual cycle

1   There are several organs in the body that secrete (produce) hormones.
Hormones are chemical messengers that are carried around the body.

Use the correct answers from the box to label the organs the produce hormones.

adrenal gland

ovary (female)

pancreas

pituitary gland

testis (male)

thyroid gland

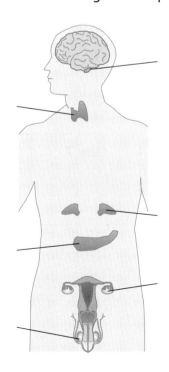

2   Hormones often affect more than one body organ. For example, the hormones associated with the menstrual cycle can affect the ovaries and the uterus at the same time.

a   How are hormones transported around the body?

_____

_____

b   What name do we use for the organs that a hormone affects?

_____

3   The menstrual cycle happens in women and girls who have been through puberty and continues until they reach the menopause at around the age of 50.
One menstrual cycle lasts for approximately 28 days.

Read the statements below.
Add the letters A–F to the correct boxes in the timeline to show the order of the menstrual cycle.

| A: Hormones cause the lining of the uterus to thicken | B: The lining of the uterus is shed. Blood and cells are lost during the period |

| C: The lining of the uterus starts to break down if the woman is not pregnant | D: The egg is released |

| E: If the egg is fertilised it will attach to the uterus wall. The menstrual cycle stops during pregnancy | F: The egg starts maturing in the ovary |

Day 1		Day 7		Day 14		Day 21

4.4 Controlling fertility

1   We can use hormones as a form of contraception for women.

Complete the box packaging below to show how this type of contraception works.

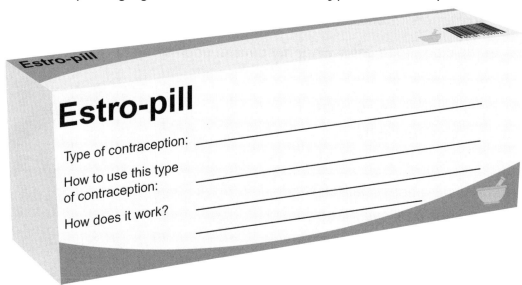

Estro-pill

Estro-pill

Type of contraception: _____

How to use this type
of contraception: _____

How does it work? _____

2   Hormones can be used for fertility treatment in women.

Which stage of the menstrual cycle do fertility treatments target,
to increase the chance of fertilisation of an egg cell?

Tick the correct stage.

A   Shedding of the lining of the uterus wall. ☐

B   Development and release of an egg cell. ☐

C   Thickening of the uterus wall. ☐

Now I know:	☹	😐	☺
The functions of the nervous system			
How a reflex arc works			
How to measure reaction time using a metre rule			
Factors that might increase or decrease reaction time			
The main stages of the menstrual cycle			
How hormonal contraception can prevent pregnancy			
How hormones can help a woman conceive (become pregnant)			

4.5 The menstrual cycle and contraception

1   Different levels of four hormones control what happens in the menstrual cycle.

Add letters to the diagram to show what happens at each stage of the cycle.

A: Follicle stimulating hormone (FSH) causes an egg to mature in the ovary

B: Follicle stimulating hormone (FSH) and luteinising hormone (LH) levels drop to normal

C: Luteinising hormone (LH) causes the egg to be released from the ovary

D: Oestrogen and progesterone cause the uterus lining to thicken

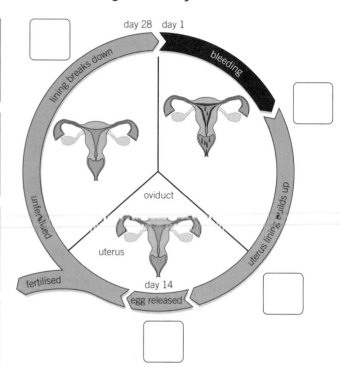

2   Look at the diagram of the menstrual cycle from question 1.

a   If you were a fertility doctor, at what time of the cycle would you advise your patient to try to get pregnant?

_____

_____

b   Why is a woman less likely to become pregnant in the first week of her menstrual cycle?

_____

3   Condoms work in a different way from oral contraceptives.

a   How does a condom prevent a woman becoming pregnant?

_____

b   What other advantages are there to using a condom for contraception over other methods?

_____

_____

4.6 Homeostasis

1 Homeostasis is important in making sure your body functions effectively.
It is the process of keeping the conditions in the body the same.

Name **two** conditions in the body that must be kept the same.

1 _____ 2 _____

2 One of the internal body conditions that must be kept the same is your blood glucose level.

People that are unable to control their blood glucose levels can have a condition called
diabetes. Diabetes can have serious health implications if not controlled.

a Look at the table below. Explain how blood glucose levels change at each event.

Event	How does the blood glucose level change?
You eat a meal	
The pancreas releases insulin. Glucose is converted to glycogen in the liver	
You exercise	

b What happens to the blood glucose level if the pancreas cannot produce enough insulin?

It would cause the blood glucose level to _____.

This would be bad for the person because _____

_____

Now I know:	☹	😐	☺
How the menstrual cycle is controlled by hormones like oestrogen and progesterone			
Other methods of contraception, including condoms			
What homeostasis is			
How blood glucose levels are kept the same in homeostasis			

Component 1: Exam-style questions

1. All organisms (living things) are made up of cells. They are the building blocks of life.

   a   The diagram shows a cell. The 'control centre' of the cell is labelled **X**.

   What is the name of this part of the cell?   **[1 mark]**

   Tick (✓) **one** box.

   Cell membrane   ☐

   Cytoplasm   ☐

   Nucleus   ☐

   b   The diagram below shows a type of specialised animal cell.

   What kind of cell is it? ....   **[1 mark]**

   c   Give **one** adaptation of the cell in part **b** that helps it perform its functions.   **[1 mark]**

   ....

2. This question is about the levels of organisation in the body.

   Use the correct answers from the box to complete the table.   **[3 marks]**

   | circulatory system | heart | nerve | nucleus | tissue |

Level of organisation	Definition	Example in human body
Cell	The smallest unit of an organism.	Muscle cell
	A group of cells with a similar structure and function.	Muscle
Organ	Made from different tissues that work together to do a job.	
Organ system	Made from a group of organs that work together to do a job.	

3. Your body is made up of many organs that have specific functions in the body.

   a Use the correct answers from the box to label the organs of the body.   **[3 marks]**

   | intestines | liver | lungs |

   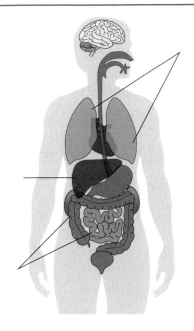

b The life choices you make can affect your health and your organs.

The column on the left shows some lifestyle choices.
The column on the right shows some effects they can have on your health and organs.

Draw **one** line from each lifestyle choice to the main effect it could have on your health or organs. **[3 marks]**

Lifestyle choice	Effect
Smoking cigarettes	Becoming overweight (obese)
Drinking large amounts of alcohol like wine or beer	Liver damage
Eating a diet with more energy in than your body needs	Lung cancer

c Regular exercise can help you to be fitter.

Which **two** of these are likely to happen because you exercise regularly? **[2 marks]**

Tick (✓) **two** boxes.

Your lungs can get bigger. ☐

Your liver will be damaged. ☐

Your body mass index is likely to be lower (and you are less likely to be obese). ☐

You are more likely to get type 2 diabetes. ☐

4. The nervous system respons to changes in your environment called stimuli.

a A reflex action is an example of a response to a stimulus.

Why are reflex actions very fast? **[1 mark]**

Tick (✓) **one** box.

The brain thinks quickly how to react. ☐

They travel around the body in the bloodstream. ☐

They travel down nerves, and don't have to go to the brain. ☐

b Name **one** reflex action. **[1 mark]**

....

5. Different foods contain different nutrients. A healthy diet contains a variety of nutrients.

Use the correct answers from the box to complete the sentences.

| carbohydrate | fats and oils |
| minerals and vitamins | protein |

a Foods like fish and lentils have a high .... content which is needed for growth and repair. **[1 mark]**

b Starchy food like bread and sugary foods like sweets are high in .... **[1 mark]**

c The table below shows the energy requirement of people of different age and sex.

Age	Male	Females
Adults	10 500 kJ	8400 kJ
18-year-olds	13 200 kJ	10 300 kJ
16-year-olds	12 400 kJ	10 100 kJ
14-year-olds	11 000 kJ	9800 kJ

Which group of people has the highest energy requirement? **[1 mark]**

....

d Why might this group of people need the most energy? **[1 mark]**

....

6. Pathogens are micoorganisms that cause disease.

a Which of these are pathogens? **[2 marks]**

Tick (✓) the correct boxes.

Bacteria ☐

Toxins ☐

Viruses ☐

White blood cells ☐

b Draw a ring around the type of cells in the body that fight pathogens. **[1 mark]**

Heart muscle cells   **Platelets**   **Red blood cells**   **White blood cells**

c Some diseases can be prevent by vaccinations.
Which of these statements about vaccination is correct? **[1 mark]**

Tick (✓) **one** box.

Vaccination can cause type 2 diabetes. ☐

When you are vaccinated, you are injected with inactive or
dead pathogens. ☐

When you are vaccinated, your body makes more platelets. ☐

d Use the correct answer from the box to complete the sentence. **[1 mark]**

antibiotics	**antibodies**	**platelets**	**red blood cells**

When you are vaccinated, your body produces ....
that help your body fight the pathogen so you don't get the disease.

7. When a girl goes through puberty, she starts her menstrual cycles.
This means that she will now be able to get pregant.

a Use the correct answers from the box to complete the sentences about
the menstrual cycle. **[3 marks]**

baby	**blood**	**hormones**	**ovaries**	**period**

The menstrual cycle occurs in women. It lasts for approximately

28 days and is controlled by ....

These chemicals travel around the body in the ....
and control the release of the egg cell.

If the egg cell is not fertilised, the woman will have a ....
at the beginning of the next cycle.

b Women who struggle to have children can be given special drugs to help by changing their menstrual cycle.
These are called infertility treatments.

Are the following statements about infertility treatments true or false?   [3 marks]

Statement	True or false?
Hormones are often given to make the ovaries release an egg cell.	
Hormones are given to prevent the egg cell being released.	
Hormones are given to make the woman have a period.	

c Some women do not want to have children. They might take the oral contraceptive pill.

Oral contraceptive pills contain hormones.
These hormones stop the ovaries releasing an egg cell.
This stops the woman taking them from getting pregnant.

Give **one** advantage and **one** disadvantage
of this type of contraception.   [2 marks]

Advantage ....

Disadvantage ....

Component 1: Exam-style questions (Trilogy)

01 **Figure 1** shows a plant cell.

Figure 1

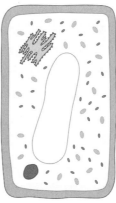

Which parts of a plant cell are **not** found in animal cells? [3 marks]

Tick **three** boxes.

Cell membrane ☐

Cell wall ☐

Chloroplasts ☐

Cytoplasm ☐

Nucleus ☐

Permanent vacuole ☐

02 Many substances move into and out of cells by a process called diffusion. This is the movement of substances from an area of high concentration to one of low concentration.

02.1 Name **two** factors that affect the rate of diffusion. [2 marks]

_____

_____

02.2 What is the name of the biological process that moves substances against their concentration gradient? [1 mark]

_____

02.3 Some cells use this process to move substances that they need across the cell membrane.
Figure **2** shows a root hair cell.

What substances are being moved by the cell in this way? [1 mark]

_____

Figure 2

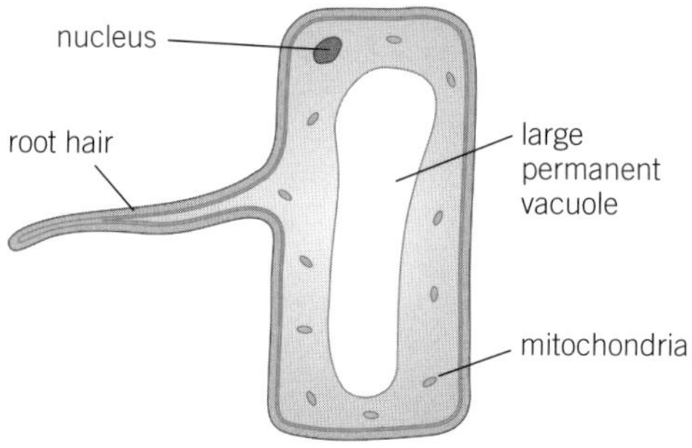

nucleus

root hair

large permanent vacuole

mitochondria

02.4 Which part of the cell provides the energy for this process? **[1 mark]**

_____

03 Amylase is a biological catalyst.
These are important chemicals for the chemical reactions in living organisms.

03.1 What term is given to biological catalysts? **[1 mark]**

_____

03.2 What does an enzyme do to a chemical reaction? **[1 mark]**

_____

_____

04.1 Complete these sentences about cardiovascular disease (CVD). **[5 marks]**

CVD affects the _____ and blood vessels.

Layers of _____ build up inside the arteries, reducing the flow of
_____ to the organs, and so they receive less _____.

The disease has a positive _____ with unhealthy diets.

04.2 Give **one** lifestyle choice apart from diet that you can change
to reduce the risk of CVD. **[1 mark]**

_____

04.3 There are various methods of treating CVD.

Draw **one** line from each treatment option to its description. **[2 marks]**

Treatment	Description
Bypass surgery	Drugs are given to reduce the rate of fatty deposits in blood vessels.
Statins	Damaged arteries replaced with vessels from other parts of the body.
Stents	A metal tube is inserted in a blood vessel to hold it open.

05 If an athlete hasn't got enough oxygen in their muscles, anaerobic respiration takes place.

05.1 What chemical would build up in the muscles instead of carbon dioxide? **[1 mark]**

Tick **one** box.

Alcohol ☐

Carbon monoxide ☐

Glucose ☐

Lactic acid ☐

05.2 How does the build-up of the chemical affect a person? **[1 mark]**

_____

05.3 After exercise, the athlete continued to breathe deeply for a while.

Give the name of the amount of oxygen that is needed to break down the lactic acid that has built up. **[1 mark]**

_____

05.4 Anaerobic respiration is useful in industry, for making bread and beer.

What is the name of this process? **[1 mark]**

_____

06 A hospital noticed that communicable diseases were being spread from patients in one ward to patients in another.

06.1 Which actions could stop the spread of disease? **[2 marks]**

Tick **two** boxes.

Cooking food thoroughly to kill bacteria present ☐

Hand washing and using alcohol gel to kill bacteria on the hands ☐

Wearing a face mask to prevent the spread of pathogens from coughs and sneezes ☐

Wiping hands with a tissue after sneezing ☐

06.2 A scientist found that two types of bacteria were responsible for the diseases being spread. In a Petri dish, they grew samples of both types of bacteria found on a contaminated mug.

Bacteria type X started with 10 bacterial cells, which divided every 20 minutes.

Bacteria type Y started with 15 cells, which divided every 30 minutes.

Calculate the final population of bacteria X and Y after one hour.

Use this formula: final population = initial population $\times 2^{\text{number of bacterial divisions}}$

[4 marks]

X: _____ Y: _____

06.3 Which type of bacteria had more cells after one hour? **[1 mark]**

_____

06.4 The scientist wanted to create a drug to treat the diseases being spread.

Name **two** features a good medicine should have. **[2 marks]**

_____

_____

07 After a woman has gone through puberty, she starts to have a menstrual cycle, which controls the release of an egg cell from the ovaries.

07.1 How often is an egg cell released?

Complete the sentence. **[1 mark]**

An egg cell is released roughly every _____ days.

07.2 Which hormones from the list are involved in controlling the menstrual cycle?

Tick **two** boxes. **[2 marks]**

Adrenaline ☐

Follicle stimulating hormone (FSH) ☐

Insulin ☐

Oestrogen ☐

Testosterone ☐

08 Hormones regulate various internal body conditions.

08.1 Which hormone reduces the level of glucose in your blood? **[1 mark]**

_____

08.2 Which body organ produces this hormone? **[1 mark]**

Tick **one** box.

Adrenal gland ☐

Ovaries ☐

Pancreas ☐

Pituitary gland ☐

08.3 The blood glucose levels of two people were tested over one day. One of the test subjects had diabetes and the other person did not. **Figure 3** shows the results.

Figure 3

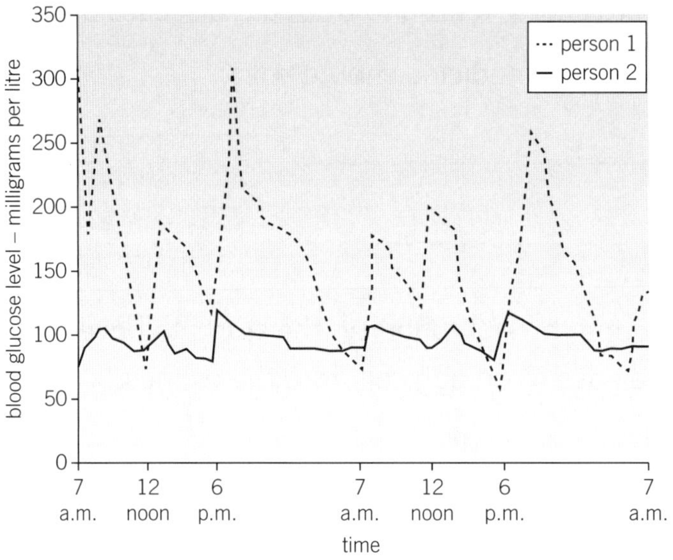

08.3 What did both test subjects do at 6 p.m.? **[1 mark]**

_____

08.4 People with diabetes do not produce the hormone in question **08.1**, and so their blood glucose levels are more unstable than in people without this condition.

Which test subject had diabetes? **[1 mark]**

Tick **one** box.

Person 1 ☐

Person 2 ☐

5 Feeding relationships

Key words

photosynthesis   reactants   products   adaptations   food chain   food web
community   population   ecosystem   decay   producer   consumer   habitat

5.1 Photosynthesis

1 Feeding relationships are very important for understanding the transfer of energy in an ecosystem.

   a What do the following terms mean when talking about feeding relationships?

   A producer is an organism that _____

   _____

   A consumer is an organism that _____

   _____

   b Sort the following organisms into producers and consumers.

Slug   Grass   Bird   Greenfly   Dandelion   Tree   Cow

Producers	Consumers

2 Photosynthesis is important for all life on Earth.

   a Complete the word equation to show what happens during photosynthesis.

   _____ + _____ $\xrightarrow{\text{light}}$ _____ + _____

   b Where does photosynthesis happen? _____

   c What is the green chemical that makes photosynthesis possible? _____

   d In a plant cell, where is this green chemical found? _____

5.2 Adaptations

1 Draw **one** line from each key word to its definition.

Habitat		A living thing

Organism		A special feature that helps an organism to survive where it lives

Adaptation		Where an organism lives

2 We know that animals and plants are adapted to survive in different conditions.

a Look at the image of a cactus.

Which adaptation helps to protect a cactus from animals that would eat it?
Tick **one** answer.

Roots that reach deep into the soil ☐

Water stored in the stem ☐

Covered in spines ☐

b Polar Bears live in the Arctic.

Draw **one** line from each adaptation to how it helps a polar bear to survive.

Adaptation	How the adaptation helps the polar bear to survive
Large feet	Camouflage
White fur	Makes fur waterproof
Greasy coat	Stops them sinking into the snow

c Look at the image of an emperor penguin.

Emperor penguins have a thick layer of fat, called blubber.

How does the layer of blubber help an Emperor penguin to survive in its habitat?

_____

_____

5.3 Food chains and food webs

1 Draw **one** line from each key word to its definition.

Ecosystem	All of the populations of organisms in an ecosystem
Population	The total number of organisms of each species in a habitat
Community	A diagram showing the feeding relationships in a community (also shows the transfer of energy)
Food chain	All of the organisms and the physical conditions in an area

2 We often use a food web (instead of a food chain) because in real life animals eat more than one thing.

The arrows show the transfer of energy when something is eaten.

Draw a food web below, including all of these organisms:

> grass   slug   bird   fox   rabbit   caterpillar   hawk   frog   grasshopper

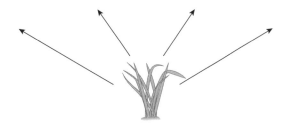

5.4 Decay

1 When animals and plants die they are broken down by a process called decay.

Other organic material like droppings and dead leaves will also decay.

Give **two** reasons why decay is important to life on Earth.

_____

_____

_____

2 Local councils encourage households to compost their dead plants
and vegetable kitchen waste by composting.

a What breaks the waste down, turning it into compost? _____

b During decay what carbon-containing gas will be released?

c What can the compost be used for when the breakdown has finished?

_____

Now I know:	☹	😐	😊
The word equation for photosynthesis			
Where photosynthesis happens			
Some ways that animals and plants are adapted to survive			
What food chains and food webs are			
Why decay is important to living things			
Some of the processes in the decay cycle			

Key words

interdependence   predator   prey   limiting factors   chlorophyll   carbon cycle

5.5 Interdependence

1 Fruit plants, like strawberries and blackberries, depend on bees for pollination.

What would happen to the numbers of fruit plants if the bees were killed and could no longer pollinate the plants?

_____

_____

_____

2 Look at the diagram below. It shows the population changes for snowshoe hares and Canadian lynx.

How are the populations of each animal interdependent?

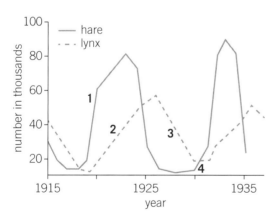

1 If the population of hares increases there is a larger food supply for the lynx.

2 This can therefore support more lynx, so more offspring survive.

3 The growing numbers of lynx eventually reduce the food supply. The number of predators starts to decrease.

4 The prey population starts to increase once more – the cycle then begins again.

As the number of hares increases, _____

_____

_____

_____

_____

_____

5.6 Factors affecting photosynthesis

1   Photosynthesis is the process by which a plant uses energy transferred from the Sun to make glucose.

The reaction doesn't always work at its fastest rate because there may be a limiting factor that prevents this.

What are the **four** limiting factors that may stop photosynthesis going at its fastest rate?

1 _____

2 _____

3 _____

4 _____

2   Look at this diagram of a leaf. It is variegated, which means that part of the leaf is white because it doesn't have any chlorophyll.

Which part of the leaf would contain starch (made of glucose) if the plant is left in sunlight?

Label the part of the leaf with starch on the diagram below.

3   Look at the graphs below. Draw on lines to show how the rate of photosynthesis is affected by light, carbon dioxide, and temperature.

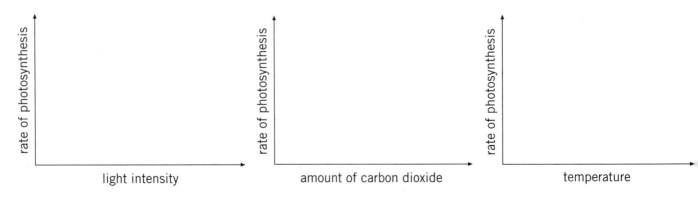

4 A farmer has a greenhouse full of tomato plants on a sunny hill in a warm part of Spain.

a Why did another farmer tell him to add a propane burner to his greenhouse?

The propane heater would burn fossil fuels

b How would this affect photosynthesis, and the growth of his tomato plants?

The rate of photosynthesis would be _____ which would lead to

_____ the growth of his tomato plants

5.7 Investigating the rate of photosynthesis

1 We can measure the rate of photosynthesis by setting up a beaker with some pondweed in it, as shown below.

When a light is placed next to the beaker and turned on, the plant starts to make bubbles of a gas. Counting the number of bubbles produced in a minute gives us a way to measure the rate of photosynthesis.

We can move the light bulb closer and further away to change the amount of light (the light intensity).

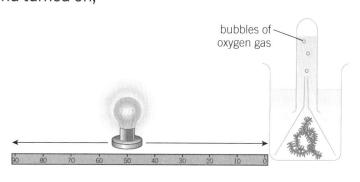

The results from this experiment are shown in the table below.

Distance from bulb (cm)	Number of bubbles produced in a minute			
	Test 1	Test 2	Test 3	Mean
0	33	40	35	
10	30	28	29	
20	25	22	22	
30	15	14	13	
40	10	11	12	

a   Calculate the mean of the results to complete the table.

b   What gas are the bubbles made of? _____

c   What happens to the number of bubbles of gas as you move the lamp away from the pondweed? _____

d   Which factor is mostly likely to be limiting in this investigation? _____

e   LED bulbs are efficient and don't get hot. Why would we try to use an LED lamp for this experiment?

_____

_____

5.8 The carbon cycle

1   The Earth's carbon is naturally recycled.

a   Name **one** way that carbon is removed from the atmosphere.

_____

b   Name **one** way that carbon is released into the atmosphere.

_____

Now I know:	☹	😐	☺
How populations of animals and plants can be interdependent			
Factors that limit the rate of photosynthesis			
How to measure the rate of photosynthesis			
The key processes in the carbon cycle			

6 Organisms and the environment

Entry Level Certificate

Key words

competition   territory   competitors   living factors   non-living factors   distribution   pollution   environment   population   quadrat   sampling

6.1 Competition

1 Competition is when animals or plants are trying to get the same resources in a habitat.

Name **three** resources that animals compete for
and **three** resources that plants compete for.

Things animals compete for:	Things plants compete for:
1 _____	1 _____
2 _____	2 _____
3 _____	3 _____

2 Circle all of the resources that an animal would **not** compete for.

Food	**Nutrients**	**Territory**
Light	**Shelter**	**Mates**

3 Circle all of the resources that a plant would **not** compete for.

Food	**Nutrients**	**Territory**
Light	**Space**	**Mates**

4 Animals and plants are adapted to help them compete.

a Many tropical rainforest plants have adapted to be tall with a wide leaf canopy.

What resource are these plants competing for?

_____

b Male deer have antlers that they use for fighting.

What factor are these animals competing for?

_____

6.2 Living and non-living factors

1 The environment changes all the time. This can affect the habitat where an animal or plant lives. These changes can be caused by living or non-living factors.

   Look at the list of changes below and decide if they are caused by living or non-living factors. Tick **one** box in each row.

	Change	Living	Non-living
A	Changes caused by extreme rainfall like flooding and erosion		
B	A new carnivore arriving in a habitat and hunting the herbivores		
C	Plants making lots of berries which would be eaten by animals		
D	A very hot summer		
E	A new competitor arriving (like rabbits arriving in Australia)		
F	A dull cloudy day with little light		

2 Climate change is causing the polar ice to melt.

   This means there is less ice for polar bears to hunt on.

   a Is this a living or non-living factor? _____

   b How might catching less prey affect the population size of the polar bears?

   _____

3 When rabbits were introduced to Australia they had no natural predators.

   a How would their arrival have affected plant populations?

   The plant populations would _____

   _____

   b How would this affect the population of other animals?

   This would cause populations of other animals to _____

   _____

6.3 Investigating plant distribution

1 A quadrat is one of the tools scientists use for sampling.

a Put the instructions in the correct order to say how you use a quadrat.

A	Count the number of dandelions in the quadrat.
B	Calculate the estimated population size = (total area ÷ sampled area) × number of dandelions counted.
C	Place your quadrat at a random location in the field.
D	Measure the area of the field you are sampling in.
E	Place the quadrat in another random location and count the dandelions again.
F	Repeat several times.

Correct order: ☐ ☐ ☐ ☐ ☐ ☐

b Which of these things would you **do** or **not do** with a quadrat? Tick **one** box in each row.

	Action	Do	Don't
A	Throw it carefully to make sure it landed on some pretty flowers		
B	Place the quadrat at intervals along a transect line		
C	Place the quadrat randomly around a field to sample the population of a plant		
D	Count plants that are outside the quadrat		

2 A group sampled along a transect line across a field. They were investigating how plants were affected by being trodden on by humans.

They found that there were fewer species of plant where humans walked on the footpath through the field.

Look at the graph below.

Which of the samples was taken on the footpath, and how can you tell?

The sample taken on the footpath was _____

_____

I know this because _____

_____

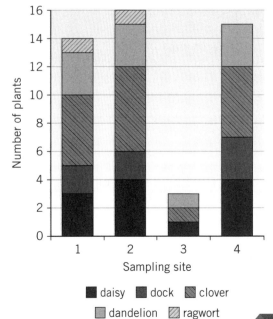

6.4 Pollution

1 Humans have effects on ecosystems. One effect is causing pollution.

Give **one** example of each type of pollution in the table below.

Land pollution	Water pollution	Air pollution

2 Look at the types of pollution below.

Say where they come from and what their effect might be.

Example	Where it comes from	Possible effect
Chemical runoff	Landfill sites	Chemicals might get into the food chain and harm animals
Pesticide		
Fertiliser in a river		
Acid rain		

Now I know:	☹	😐	☺
The things animals and plants compete for in a habitat			
The living and non-living factors that affect communities			
How to measure populations of plants with a quadrat			
How pollution can affect populations			
Some examples of different types of pollution			

biodiversity   deforestation   agriculture   conservation
breeding programme   green corridor

6.5 Loss of biodiversity

1 Biodiversity is a measure of the number of different species of living organism in a place. In general, the greater the biodiversity, the healthier the environment is.

The factors below lead to a decrease or an increase in biodiversity.

Complete the table to show the effect of each factor on biodiversity.

Tick **one** box in each row.

	Action	Increase biodiversity	Decrease biodiversity
A	Deforestation (removal of large areas of forest)		
B	Agriculture (modern farming techniques)		
C	Planting a selection of native trees on ex-industrial land		
D	Hedgerow planting to provide hedges between fields		
E	Pollution		
F	Encouraging gardeners to plant more nectar-bearing flowers		

2 Scientists often disagree with fishermen over how many fish can be caught off the coast of the United Kingdom.

Scientists argue that catching too many fish will change the biodiversity of our fish stocks.

a How might the number of types of fish change?

_____

b How could the number of types of fish be changed by pollution, such as the release of raw sewage into the sea?

_____

6.6 Maintaining biodiversity

1 We try to conserve species to prevent them from becoming extinct.

What does it mean when a species becomes extinct?

_____

2 Green corridors are being planted around the world.
These are areas of nature that connect one habitat to another.

a How will planting green corridors affect biodiversity?

Green corridors will _____

b Why will this happen?

This will happen because _____

_____

3 Lots of zoos in the UK are part of international breeding programmes.

a What does the term 'breeding programme' mean?

A breeding programme takes animals that are _____

_____

b Running a successful breeding programme requires a lot of expertise and resources.

Give **two** difficulties of running a successful breeding programme.

1 _____

2 _____

Now I know:	☹	😐	🙂
What biodiversity is			
Some of the factors that can decrease biodiversity			
Things we can do to increase biodiversity			

7 How life developed on Earth

Entry Level Certificate

Key words

DNA   double helix   inherit   chromosomes   genes   alleles
reproduction   sexual   asexual   clone   variation   evolution
natural selection   fossils   artificial selection (selective breeding)

7.1 Genetic material

1 DNA is an important chemical that contains the information needed to make an organism.

Where is DNA found in a cell? Circle **one** answer.

cytoplasm   membrane   nucleus   vacuole

2 The genetic material in humans determines characteristics, like hair colour.

Draw **one** line from each genetic component to its description.

Genetic component	Description
DNA	Long strands of DNA, organised in pairs
Chromosomes	A long molecule that contains the information needed to make an organism
Genes	Short sections of DNA that carry a specific piece of information

3 Different organisms contain different numbers of chromosomes.

Complete these questions about chromosomes in humans.

a How many pairs of chromosomes does a human have? _____

b What is the total number of chromosomes found in a human? _____

c How many sex chromosomes does a human have? _____

d If someone had XY sex chromosomes, what sex would they be? _____

7.2 Asexual and sexual reproduction

1 Asexual and sexual reproduction can be found in the animal and plant world.

Circle the features of asexual reproduction.
Underline the features of sexual reproduction.

Needs two parents

The offspring contains DNA from 1 parent

The offspring is genetically identical to its parent

The offspring contains DNA from 2 parents

Likely to show variation

Unlikely to show variation

The offspring is different from both parents

Only one parent needed

2 Give an example of sexual reproduction. Refer to gametes in your answer.

_____

3 Asexual reproduction produces a clone. What is a clone?

_____

4 Plants like spider plants and strawberry plants reproduce by putting down runners.

a Which type of reproduction is this?

_____

b Would the offspring look the same as their parent plant, or different?

_____

7.3 Investigating variation

1 Variation is the differences between members of the same species.

Identify which of the following differences are inherited and which ones are environmental.
Tick **one** box in each row.

Difference	Inherited	Environmental
A tattoo		
Blonde hair		
A scar		
Detached earlobes		
Eye colour		

2 A student wanted to see if there was a relationship between the height and shoe size of his classmates. Here are the results.

Shoe size of person	7	8	10	9	8	10	11	5	12	6	8	7
Height of person (cm)	169	168	177	173	168	178	182	160	183	166	170	163

a Plot the results on the graph paper below.

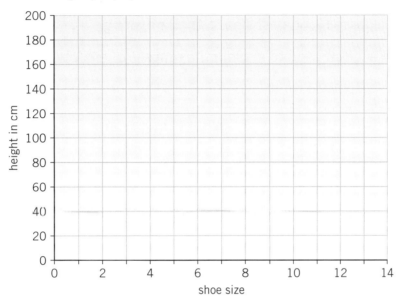

b Look at the relationship diagrams below.

Which one is most like your graph? Tick **one** box.

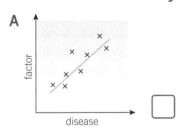
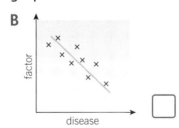
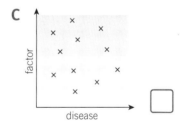

c Look at your graph. Describe the relationship between height and shoe size.

_____

7.4 Evolution and natural selection

1 Charles Darwin was one of the first scientists to put forward an idea of how evolution might work.

What did he call his theory? _____

2   Which of these theories is the best summary of Darwin's theory? Tick **one** box.

    A   Giraffes stretched their necks to reach food. They passed
       on their longer necks to their offspring. ☐

    B   Giraffes with longer necks could reach more food so more
       survived to pass on longer necks to their offspring. ☐

    C   Giraffes with long necks were attracted to other giraffes with
       long necks. They passed long necks on to their offspring. ☐

3   The peppered moth is often used to explain the process of evolution.

    a   Put the stages of peppered moth evolution into the correct order.

Stage	What is happening
A	After the industrial revolution, the trees lost their pollution (soot). Birds ate the black moths. There were more white moths than black again.
B	The industrial revolution happened and trees were covered in pollution (soot). The black moths were camouflaged but the white moths could be spotted easily. Birds ate the white moths instead.
C	Most of the peppered moths were light in colour. They were camouflaged because the trees were light in colour (covered in lichens). Birds ate the black moths because they were easier to see.
D	There were now more black moths than white moths.

    Correct order: ☐☐☐☐

    b   What happened to the colour of the tree bark during the
       industrial revolution (stages B and C)? _____

    c   Why are there more white moths now?

    _____

4   We have evidence from the fossil record to support the theory of evolution.

Complete the table to show which statements are true and which ones are false.

	Statement	True or false?
A	The oldest fossils are found at the surface.	
B	Fossils are the soft remains of an animal, such as muscle.	
C	Fossils are found in igneous rocks (formed in volcanoes).	
D	Fossils are imprints of where a dead animal or plant would have been.	
E	Fossils are usually found in sedimentary rock.	

7.5 Artificial selection

1   A breeder uses selective breeding to create a pedigree dog with the characteristics he is looking for.

Put these steps into the correct order.

A   The breeder would do this repeatedly to get the perfect dog.

B   The breeder would breed those animals with other animals showing the same characteristics.

C   The breeder would choose the offspring that show the best characteristics.

D   The breeder would select dogs that had the characteristics he was looking for.

E   The breeder would breed these animals again with other similar dogs.

Correct order: ☐☐☐☐☐

2   Farmers also selectively breed plants that they grow for food.

List **two** traits that a farmer might want to select for.

1 _____

2 _____

3   It takes many generations of breeding (the farmer must do it over and over) to get the desired characteristics. Why can't the farmer just do it once?

In only one generation of breeding, the farmer would only see

_____

_____

7.6 Genetic engineering

1   Genetic engineering is not the same as selective breeding.

Complete the following sentences by filling in the blanks and circling the correct words.

Genetic engineering involves directly changing _____, altering the DNA of a living thing. It is quite a **quick / slow** process.

Artificial selection (selective breeding) involves breeding plants or animals that have the _____ you want. It is a **quick / slow** process.

In both genetic engineering and artificial selection, you end up producing an organism with **the same / different** characteristics.

2   Genetic engineering can be very useful, but it can also be risky.

Name **one** benefit and **one** risk of genetic engineering.

Benefit: _____

_____

Risk: _____

_____

Now I know:	☹	😐	☺
Where DNA is found and what it looks like (its structure)			
The difference between asexual and sexual reproduction			
What a clone is			
The difference between inherited and environmental variation			
How organisms that were suited to their environment survived, and those that were not became extinct			
What a fossil is			
How artificial selection (selective breeding) can be used to create crops or livestock with characteristics useful to humans			
What genetic engineering is			

Key words

dominant   recessive   characteristic   homozygous   heterozygous
phenotype   genotype   Punnett square   genetic cross

7.7 Dominant and recessive alleles

1   Draw **one** line from each key word to its definition.

Key word	Definition
Gene	A gene that needs two copies of the same allele for the characteristic to be expressed (shown) in the organism.
Allele	These control the different characteristics of an organism, for example eye colour and hair colour.
Dominant	A gene that only needs one copy of an allele for the characteristic to be expressed (shown) in the organism.
Recessive	Different versions of the same gene. For example, a person might have a version for blue eyes and a version for brown eyes.

2   In the table below, the genes **B** and **b** control hair colour.
The dominant allele is brown hair (**B**) and the allele for blonde hair is recessive (**b**).

Complete the table to predict the hair colour of the person and
say if the person is homozygous or heterozygous.

Combination of alleles	Predicted hair colour	Homozygous or heterozygous?
BB		
Bb		
bb		

3   Write a simple definition for phenotype and genotype (use the word in a sentence).

The genotype is the combination of _____

_____

The phenotype is the observable _____

_____

7.8 Genetic crosses

1 Whether someone is male or female is controlled by a single pair of chromosomes.

What sex would a person with the following combinations of genes be?

a XX _____

b XY _____

2 Cystic fibrosis is a recessive genetic disease that can be inherited.

F is the healthy allele, and **f** is the recessive cystic fibrosis allele.

a Two parents who both carry the cystic fibrosis allele (**Ff**) have a baby.

Complete the Punnett square.

Mother

Father

b Count the combinations and complete the table below.

Genotype (combination of alleles)	Probability of getting this genotype	Probability as a percentage
FF	/4	%
Ff	/4	%
ff	/4	%

c What is the chance of the baby inheriting cystic fibrosis? _____%

d What is their chance of having a healthy baby without cystic fibrosis? _____%

Now I know:	🙁	😐	🙂
What an allele is			
The difference between dominant and recessive alleles			
What the words phenotype and genotype mean			
What it means to be heterozygous and homozygous			
How to show a genetic cross using a Punnett square			

Component 2: Exam-style questions

1. a What is the name of the process by which plants and algae make their food?   **[1 mark]**

   ....

   b What is one substance that is produced in this process?   **[1 mark]**

   Tick (✓) **one** box.

   carbon dioxide ☐

   light ☐

   oxygen ☐

2. The photo shows an elephant.

   Draw **one** line from each adaptation of an elephant
   to the explanation of how it helps elephants to survive.   **[2 marks]**

Adaptation	How it helps elephants to survive
Long trunk	Reach food in high branches and on the ground
Tusks	Flap to keep cool in hot weather
Large ears	Strip bark from trees for food

3. Look at this food chain. It starts with a plant and ends with a snake.

   Plant → Grasshopper → Frog → Snake

   a Which statement about this food chain is true?   **[1 mark]**

   Tick (✓) **one** box.

   The frog eats the grasshopper. ☐

   The grasshopper is a predator. ☐

   The snake eats the grasshopper. ☐

b Which organism in the diagram is a producer? **[1 mark]**

....

C A food web shows how lots of different food chains are linked.

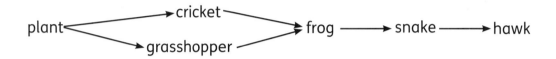

Shrews eat grasshoppers and are eaten by snakes and hawks.

Add a shrew onto the diagram to complete the food web. **[3 marks]**

d Complete the sentence. **[1 mark]**

Snakes and hawks both eat shrews.
This means they are .... for food.

4. Use the correct answers from the box to complete each sentence. **[3 marks]**

a The energy for photosynthesis comes from the ....

b The process that returns carbon dioxide to the atmosphere from

dead animals and plants is called ....

c Changes to the population of one organism affects the population
of the others.

The term for how organism populations are linked is ....

5. A gardener removes the weeds from their garden to reduce competition between their plants and weeds.

   Draw a ring around the thing plants and weeds compete for. **[1 mark]**

         herbicide   mates   oxygen   space

6. Which factors below are non-living factors? **[2 marks]**

   Tick (✓) **two** boxes.

   Air temperature ☐

   Competition from another species ☐

   Increased rainfall ☐

   Presence of predators ☐

7. Which gas causes acid rain? **[1 mark]**

   Tick (✓) **one** box.

   Methane ☐

   Nitrogen ☐

   Sulfur dioxide ☐

8. Human activities affect the environment.

   The column on the left shows some human activities.

   The column on the right shows some effects on the environment.

   Draw **one** line from each activity to the effect it can have on the environment. **[2 marks]**

Activity	Effect
Cars driving down a road	Pollution in streams that are near the fields
Spraying herbicide on crops to kill weeds	Produces gases that cause acid rain
A local picnic spot	Litter is dropped

9. Put the following in order of size from smallest to largest.

   The first one has been done for you. **[3 marks]**

   | cell | chromosome | nucleus | ~~gene~~ |

   gene ....

10. Use the correct answer from the box to complete each sentence. **[3 marks]**

    | natural selection | evolution | genetic engineering |
    | sexual selection | less | more | artificial selection |

    The theory of .... states that all living organisms
    developed from simple life forms.
    This occurred through a process called ....
    Individuals with characteristics that are best suited to their habitat
    are .... likely to survive, breed, and pass on
    the characteristic.

11. The sex chromosomes control if a baby will be male or female.

    Which sex are the following babies? **[2 marks]**

    a XX: ....

    b XY: ....

12. Which of the following is the true statement about selective breeding? **[1 mark]**

    Tick (✓) **one** box.

    Darwin wrote about selective breeding when he saw
    finches with different beak shapes. ☐

    Farmers can breed animals like cows to have bigger
    muscles (more meat). ☐

    When trees were sooty, dark peppered moths became
    more common by selective breeding. ☐

01.1 **Figure 1** shows the processes in the carbon cycle.

Figure 1

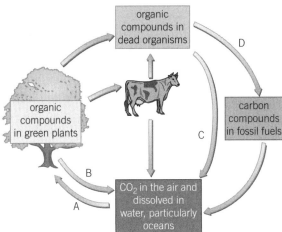

Complete the table with the letters in the diagram to name each process. **[3 marks]**

Respiration	
Decay	
Photosynthesis	
Fossil fuel formation	

01.2 Describe how the process of decay moves carbon from organisms to the atmosphere. **[2 marks]**

_____

_____

02.1 Which of these statements correctly defines biodiversity? **[1 mark]**

Tick **one** box.

The total mass of living things in an area. ☐

The total number of living individual organisms in an area. ☐

The number of different species of living organisms in an area. ☐

How much crop you can harvest from an area ☐

02.2 Human activity can cause a loss of biodiversity in an ecosystem.

Draw **one** line from each human activity
to the effect it can have on the environment. **[3 marks]**

Activity	Effect
Burning fossil fuels to release sulfur dioxide and nitrogen oxides	Acid rain
Using pesticides in fields	Habitat destruction
Digging up peat for gardening	Pollutes local waterways
An increase in the population of a town	Creates more rubbish/waste

02.3 Describe how breeding programmes can help maintain biodiversity. **[2 marks]**

_____

_____

03 In the inheritance of characteristics like hair colour, one allele will often produce a characteristic even though there is only one copy of the allele.

What is the name given to this kind of allele? **[1 mark]**

Tick **one** box.

Dominant ☐

Recessive ☐

04 Giraffe cells have 62 chromosomes.

How many chromosomes are in a sperm cell of a giraffe?

Tick **one** box. **[1 mark]**

31 ☐

62 ☐

93 ☐

124 ☐

05   Describe how a racehorse breeder could use selective breeding
to produce horses that are fast and have stamina over long distances.   **[5 marks]**

_____

_____

_____

_____

_____

_____

06   **Figure 2** shows a food web.

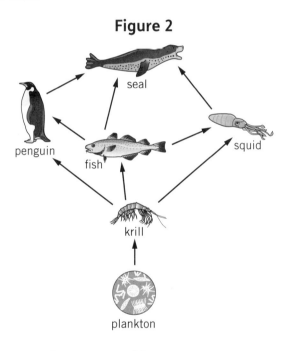

Figure 2

06.1   Name a species that is a predator to squid.   **[1 mark]**

_____

06.2   Explain how the population of squid will change
if the population of krill increases.   **[2 marks]**

_____

_____

06.3 Figure 3 shows how the population of seals has changed over fifty years.

Figure 3

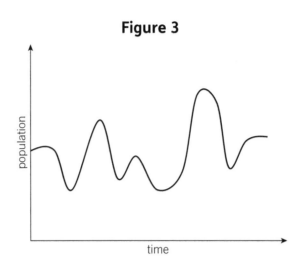

Draw the population of fish on the same axes.   **[3 marks]**

06.4 Name **one** thing that the penguin might compete for as well as food.   **[1 mark]**

_____

06.5 Describe **one** effect on the whole ecosystem shown in the food web if seals were hunted to extinction.
Consider the **whole** system rather than individual species.   **[2 marks]**

_____

_____

07 Students carried out an investigation into the effect of temperature on the rate of photosynthesis of a plant.
They measured the volume of oxygen the plant produced in 15 minutes.

07.1 Complete the sentence.

The greater the volume of oxygen produced in 15 minutes,
the _____ the rate of photosynthesis.   **[1 mark]**

07.2 The student's results are given in the table.

Temperature in °C	Volume of oxygen produced in mm³
0	120
10	200
20	270
30	330
40	360
50	0

Use the axes below to plot the student's data.   [2 marks]

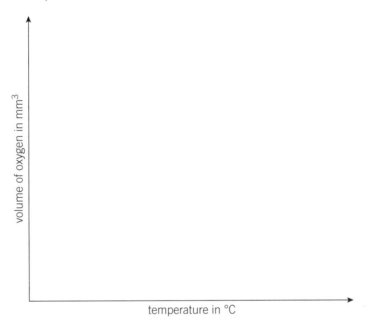

07.3 Explain why the rate of photosynthesis drops after 40 °C.   [2 marks]

_____

_____

07.4 Name **one** other factor that affects the rate of photosynthesis.   [1 mark]

_____

07.5 Identify the part of a plant cell where photosynthesis occurs.

Tick **one** box. **[1 mark]**

Cell wall ☐

Chloroplast ☐

Cytoplasm ☐

Nucleus ☐

08 The inheritance of sex in humans is determined by genetics.

Females always have two **X** sex chromosomes.
Males have one **X** and one **Y** chromosome.

08.1 Complete the Punnett square below. **[4 marks]**

Chromosomes
from the father

		X	Y
Chromosomes from the mother	X		
	X		

08.2 What is the chance of having a male baby (XY)? _____ **[1 mark]**

08.3 What is the chance of having a female baby (XX)? _____ **[1 mark]**

08.4 A mother has two daughters.

Give **two** reasons why these children look different from each other. **[2 marks]**

_____

_____

8 Atoms, elements, and compounds

Key words

atoms   elements   periodic table   groups   periods   metals   non-metals   alkali metals   halogens   compounds   chemical reaction   word equation

8.1 Atoms and the periodic table

1   All substances are made of particles so small you can't see them with your eyes or a microscope.

Name these particles. _____

2   The periodic table contains all the elements.

a   What is an element?

Elements only have _____

b   The periodic table groups similar elements together.
Add the group numbers 0 to 7 to the periodic table below.

		key				1 **H** hydrogen 1													4 **He** helium 2
7 **Li** lithium 3	9 **Be** beryllium 4		relative atomic mass **atomic symbol** name atomic (proton) number									11 **B** boron 5	12 **C** carbon 6	14 **N** nitrogen 7	16 **O** oxygen 8	19 **F** fluorine 9	20 **Ne** neon 10		
23 **Na** sodium 11	24 **Mg** magnesium 12											27 **Al** aluminium 13	28 **Si** silicon 14	31 **P** phosphorus 15	32 **S** sulfur 16	35.5 **Cl** chlorine 17	40 **Ar** argon 18		
39 **K** potassium 19	40 **Ca** calcium 20	45 **Sc** scandium 21	48 **Ti** titanium 22	51 **V** vanadium 23	52 **Cr** chromium 24	55 **Mn** manganese 25	56 **Fe** iron 26	59 **Co** cobalt 27	59 **Ni** nickel 28	63.5 **Cu** copper 29	65 **Zn** zinc 30	70 **Ga** gallium 31	73 **Ge** germanium 32	75 **As** arsenic 33	79 **Se** selenium 34	80 **Br** bromine 35	84 **Kr** krypton 36
85 **Rb** rubidium 37	88 **Sr** strontium 38	89 **Y** yttrium 39	91 **Zr** zirconium 40	93 **Nb** niobium 41	96 **Mo** molybdenum 42	[98] **Tc** technetium 43	101 **Ru** ruthenium 44	103 **Rh** rhodium 45	106 **Pd** palladium 46	108 **Ag** silver 47	112 **Cd** cadmium 48	115 **In** indium 49	119 **Sn** tin 50	122 **Sb** antimony 51	128 **Te** tellurium 52	127 **I** iodine 53	131 **Xe** xenon 54
133 **Cs** caesium 55	137 **Ba** barium 56	139 **La*** lanthanum 57	178 **Hf** hafnium 72	181 **Ta** tantalum 73	184 **W** tungsten 74	186 **Re** rhenium 75	190 **Os** osmium 76	192 **Ir** iridium 77	195 **Pt** platinum 78	197 **Au** gold 79	201 **Hg** mercury 80	204 **Tl** thallium 81	207 **Pb** lead 82	209 **Bi** bismuth 83	[209] **Po** polonium 84	[210] **At** astatine 85	[222] **Rn** radon 86
[223] **Fr** francium 87	[226] **Ra** radium 88	[227] **Ac*** actinium 89	[261] **Rf** rutherfordium 104	[262] **Db** dubnium 105	[266] **Sg** seaborgium 106	[264] **Bh** bohrium 107	[277] **Hs** hassium 108	[268] **Mt** meitnerium 109	[271] **Ds** darmstadtium 110	[272] **Rg** roentgenium 111	[285] **Cn** copernicium 112	[286] **Nh** nihonium 113	[289] **Fl** flerovium 114	[289] **Mc** moscovium 115	[293] **Lv** livermorium 116	[294] **Ts** tennessine 117	[294] **Og** oganesson 118

c   Colour in all of the metals in the periodic table above.

d   Which group is chlorine (Cl) in? _____

e   Which group is potassium (K) in? _____

f   Is boron (B) a metal or a non-metal? _____

8.2 Groups in the periodic table

1 In the periodic table, elements with similar properties are in the same group.

    a Which group contains the alkali metals? _____

    b Which group contains the halogens? _____

2 Which gas is produced when an alkali metal reacts with water? _____

3 Draw an arrow next to the following elements to show which way the reactivity **increases**.

    a The alkali metals

| 7 |
| Li |
| lithium |
| 3 |

| 23 |
| Na |
| sodium |
| 11 |

| 39 |
| K |
| potassium |
| 19 |

| 85 |
| Rb |
| rubidium |
| 37 |

| 133 |
| Cs |
| caesium |
| 55 |

| [223] |
| Fr |
| francium |
| 87 |

    b The halogens

| 19 |
| F |
| fluorine |
| 9 |

| 35.5 |
| Cl |
| chlorine |
| 17 |

| 80 |
| Br |
| bromine |
| 35 |

| 127 |
| I |
| iodine |
| 53 |

| [210] |
| At |
| astatine |
| 85 |

8.3 Making compounds

1 Which of these is the correct definition of a compound?

Tick the correct statement.

    A More than one type of element mixed together. ☐

    B More than one type of element chemically joined together. ☐

    C A compound always includes a metal and a non-metal. ☐

2 For each diagram, write if it is an element or a compound.

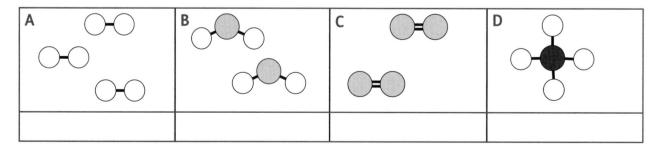

3 Complete the word equations for the following reactions.

   a Sodium + oxygen → _____

   b Magnesium + oxygen → _____

   c Iron + sulfur → _____

4 a Complete the table below to show how the names of these compounds end.

      Two have been done for you.

Non-metal element(s) in compound	End of name in compound
oxygen	oxide
sulfur	
chlorine	
bromine	
sulfur and oxygen	sulfate
nitrogen and oxygen	

   b Name the compounds that would be formed from the elements in the table.

Elements in the compound	Name of the compound
iron, sulfur, and oxygen	
magnesium and chlorine	
lithium and bromine	
potassium, nitrogen, and oxygen	

Now I know:	☹	😐	☺
Which sides of the periodic table metals and non-metals are found on			
What an element and a compound are			
Where to find groups 1 and 7 on the periodic table			
How the reactivity changes as you go down group 1 and group 7			
How to write a word equation for a simple reaction (for example, a metal burning in oxygen)			
How to name simple compounds like chlorides and sulfates			

Key words

relative mass   isotope   electrons   protons   neutrons   ions   displacement

8.4 The model of the atom

1 Use the words in the box to label the diagram of an atom.

electron   neutron   nucleus   proton

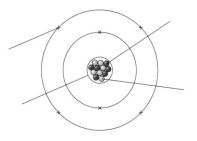

2 Draw **one** line to match each subatomic particle to its charge and its mass.

Type of sub-atomic particle	Relative charge	Relative mass
electron	+1	1
neutron	−1	very small
proton	0	1

3 For each of the atoms below, write how many protons and neutrons there are.

Element	Number of protons	Number of neutrons
24 Mg 12		
19 F 9		
14 Ne 7		

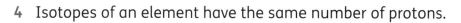

4   Isotopes of an element have the same number of protons.

The diagrams below show the isotopes of hydrogen.

How are isotopes of an element different?

The isotopes of an element have a different number of _____ but _____

_____

8.5 Atoms and elements

1   The first (inner) shell of an atom can hold up to 2 electrons and
the second shell can hold up to 8 electrons.

Complete the diagram below to show the electron structure for fluorine.
Use the information in the fluorine box from the periodic table to help you.

| 19 |
| F |
| 9 |

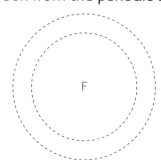

2   You should know the electronic structures of the first twenty elements of the periodic table.

Complete the table below.

Element	Number of protons/electrons	1st electron shell	2nd electron shell	3rd electron shell
sodium	11			
oxygen	8			
chlorine	17			
lithium	3			
potassium	19			

3   What is the link between the electronic structure of an element and its position in the periodic table?

_____

8.6 Metals and the periodic table

1 Which side of the periodic table are the metals on? _____

2 Name **two** properties that metals have in common.

1 _____   2 _____

3 Metals react by losing electrons from their outer shell, becoming a charged particle.

   a What is the name of these charged particles? _____

   b When magnesium reacts, it loses two electrons from its outer shell.

      What is the charge of the magnesium ion after it has lost these two negative particles? Circle the correct option.

      −2   −1   0   +1   +2

   c This is a sodium atom before it reacts.

      Draw the charged particle that is produced when sodium reacts. (Sodium loses one electron.)

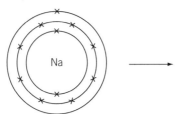

4 Why do the metals in group 1 become more reactive as you go down the group?

Because the atoms get _____

8.7 Non-metals and the periodic table

1 Which side of the periodic table are the non-metals on? _____

2 Name **two** properties that non-metals often have in common.

1 _____   2 _____

3 This is an atom of chlorine.

   Draw the ion that is produced when chlorine reacts with a metal. (Chlorine gains one electron.)

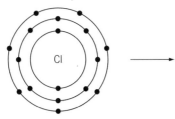

4 The reactivity of group 7 elements changes as you go down the group, because it is more difficult for the atoms to gain an electron.

Which elements are most reactive? Tick the correct option.

top of group 7 ☐   bottom of group 7 ☐

5   More reactive halogens can displace (take the place of) less reactive halogens. We call these displacement reactions.

Name the chemicals present after the substances below have been allowed time to react.

Use the reactivity order of the halogen boxes from the periodic table to help you.

| 19 |
| **F** |
| fluorine |
| 9 |

| 35 |
| **Cl** |
| chlorine |
| 17 |

| 80 |
| **Br** |
| bromine |
| 35 |

| 127 |
| **I** |
| iodine |
| 53 |

| 210 |
| **At** |
| astatine |
| 85 |

Reactivity decreases down the group

Present at the start of the reaction	Present at the end of the reaction
Potassium bromide and chlorine	Potassium chloride and
Sodium iodide and bromine	
Magnesium bromide and fluorine	

Now I know:	☹	😐	☺
The subatomic particles that make up an ion			
Where to find the atomic number and mass number on the periodic table			
What an isotope is			
How electrons are arranged in shells (for the first twenty elements)			
General properties of metals and non-metals			
The ions formed by group 1 metals			
The ions formed by group 7 non-metals			
How to predict if a displacement reaction will occur between a halogen and a compound containing a different halogen			

9 Mixtures and compounds

Key words

states of matter   solid   liquid   gas   evaporation   condensation   melting   freezing   mixture   filtration   distillation   crystallisation   chromatography   polymer   biodegradable   monomer

9.1 States of matter

1   Draw **one** line from each state to the correct diagram and description.

State of matter	Particle diagram	Description
Solids	**X** *(particle diagram)*	The particles are not touching. There is space between them and they move about in all directions
Liquids	**Y** *(particle diagram)*	Particles are touching and arranged in a regular pattern. They are fixed in place and cannot move about, only vibrate
Gases	**Z** *(particle diagram)*	Particles are touching but are NOT arranged in a regular pattern. They are able to move about and change place

2   Name each of the following changes of state.

   a   Solid to liquid: _____

   b   Gas to liquid: _____

   c   Liquid to solid: _____

   d   Liquid to gas: _____

3 Most metals have a high melting point and most non-metals have a low melting point.

What does this tell us about the forces that hold their particles together?

The forces between particles in a metal must be _____

because _____

The forces between particles in a non-metal must be _____

because _____

9.2 Mixtures

1 a Which of these diagrams shows a mixture? Tick the correct diagram.

A

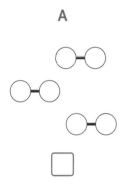

□

B

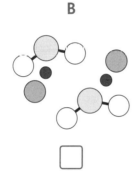

□

C

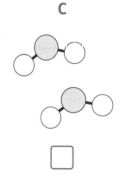

□

b How did you decide this one was a mixture?

_____

2 We can separate a solid from a liquid using a technique called filtration.
The diagram below shows sand being filtered from water.

Add the following labels to the diagram.

> Filtrate (water)   Filter paper   Funnel   Residue (sand)

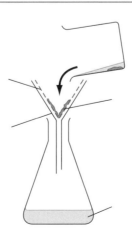

3 During crystallisation, where does the liquid go from the salt solution?

_____

_____

salt solution
evaporating dish
water
x x x x x x x x x x x
heat

4 Name the separation techniques you would use to separate the following substances.

a Water from ink: _____

b Copper sulfate from copper sulfate solution: _____

c Water and chalk: _____

d Sand and salt water: _____

9.3 Chromatography

1 We can separate substances in a solution using chromatography.

Draw lines to match each chromatography term to its definition.

Term	Definition
Solvent	The substance that is dissolved
Solute	Where the liquid has moved to up the filter paper
Solvent front	The liquid the substance is dissolved in
Chromatogram	The solute dissolved in the solvent
Solution	The piece of paper left (the result) of a chromatography experiment

2 Why do you use a pencil and not pen for drawing the line at the bottom of the chromatography paper?

_____

3 Look at the results from a chromatogram of lipstick.

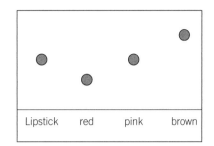

Which colour does the lipstick contain? _____

9.4 Structures of carbon

1 Diamond and graphite are both made of only carbon atoms, but they have very different structures.

   a Name the structures below:

X

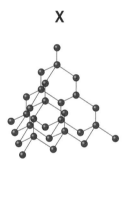

Y

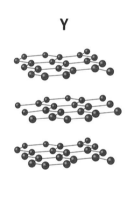

_____

_____

   b Give **three** properties of these structures.

     X: _____

     _____

     Y: _____

     _____

2 Drill bits are often coated in diamond. What makes diamond good for this purpose?

_____

3 Graphite is often used as a lubricant. What makes graphite good for this purpose?

_____

9.5 Polymers

1 Draw the polymer for each of these monomers.

a

b

2 Tick the correct boxes to show which polymer properties are advantages and which are disadvantages.

	Property	Advantage	Disadvantage
A	They can easily be moulded into different shapes		
B	They are not biodegradable and do not rot		
C	They are cheap and easy to produce		
D	They are unreactive and resistant to chemicals		

3 We are finding lots of very small pieces of plastic (microplastics) in sea creatures.

Which property of polymers leads to them being found in sea creatures?

_____

Now I know:	☹	😐	☺
The names and properties of the states of matter			
The names of the changes of state			
What a mixture is			
How mixtures can be separated by filtration			
How mixtures can be separated by distillation			
How the different solutes in a solution can be identified by chromatography			
The structures and properties of diamond and graphite			
The structure and properties of polymers			

Key words

| pure substance | formulation | concentration | covalent | ionic | lattice |

9.6 Pure substances and formulations

1 A student boiled three samples of water.
   Which sample of water was pure?

   Tick **one** box.

   A boiled at 102°C ☐   B boiled at 101°C ☐   C boiled at 100°C ☐

2 A student heated two different substances and measured the temperatures as they cooled
   to room temperature. The graph shows the results.

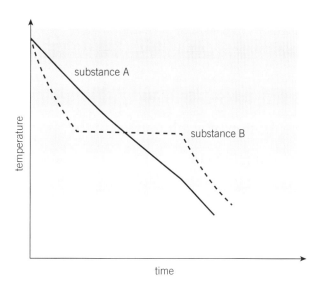

   a Which substance is likely to be pure? _____

   b How can you tell?

      This substance will freeze (turn to a solid) at _____

3 A formulation is a mixture of substances.

   They are mixed to do a specific job and make a useful product.

   Give **one** example of a formulation. _____

9.7 Concentration

1 The concentration of a solution tells us how much solute is dissolved in a certain volume of liquid.

The diagrams below show three different concentrations of solution.

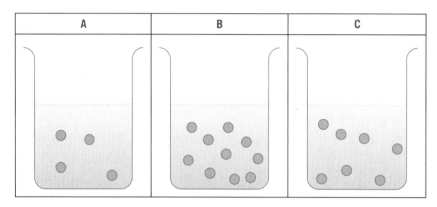

Which solution has the highest concentration? Explain how you can tell.

The solution with the highest concentration is _____

I can tell because it has the most _____

_____

2 We can calculate the concentration of a solution using the formula:

$$\text{concentration (g/dm}^3) = \frac{\text{mass of solute (g)}}{\text{volume of solution (dm}^3)}$$

Calculate the concentration if 50 g of copper sulfate is dissolved in 2 dm³ of water.

_____ g/dm³

3 Sometimes we need to calculate the mass of solute that is dissolved in a solution.

We can use the formula:

Mass of solute (g) = concentration (g/dm³) × volume of solution (dm³)

Calculate the amount of salt (sodium chloride) you can get from salt water with a concentration of 50 g/dm³.
The volume of the salt water is 4 dm³.

_____ g

9.8 Covalent molecules

1 Covalent bonds are formed between non-metal elements.

    a Which of the compounds below are likely to have covalent bonds?
Tick the correct boxes.

Carbon dioxide ☐   Aluminium oxide ☐   Oxygen ☐

Copper sulfate ☐   Methane (CH_4) ☐   Sodium chloride ☐

    b Complete a dot and cross diagram for a molecule of nitrogen, which contains 2 atoms of nitrogen (atomic number 7, which has the electronic structure 2,5).

2 List the properties you expect a covalent compound with small molecules to have.

The electrical conductivity as a solid or liquid would be _____

The melting and boiling points would be _____

3 a Name a substance that has a giant covalent structure. _____

    b Draw its structure.

9.9 Ionic compounds

1 Ionic compounds contain a metal and a non-metal element that have bonded together.

Which of the compounds beloware likely to have ionic bonds?
Tick the correct boxes.

Carbon dioxide ☐   Iron oxide ☐   Water ☐

Copper sulfate ☐   Methane (CH_4) ☐   Sodium chloride ☐

2 The ions in an ionic compound have a full outer shell of electrons and have either a positive charge (metals) or negative charge (non-metals).

Draw the ions produced when magnesium reacts with oxygen.

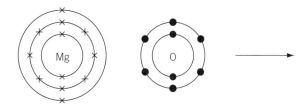

3 List the properties you expect anionic compounds with small molecules to have.

The electrical conductivity when melted or dissolved would be

The melting and boiling points would be

4 Draw a simple diagram to show the lattice structure of a compound with ionic bonding. Use the ion symbols shown on the right in your diagram.

Now I know:	🙁	😐	🙂
What a pure substance is			
How to identify a pure substance by the melting or boiling point			
What a formulation is			
What concentration is			
How to use the formula for concentration to do some simple calculations			
What happens to the electrons in a covalent and ionic bond			
The properties of chemicals with covalent and ionic bonds			

10 Metals and Alloys

Entry Level Certificate

Key words

conductor   density   corrosion   ore   extraction   recycling   alloy

10.1 Metals

1 a Tick the side of the periodic table where you find metals. Tick **one** box.

left ☐   right ☐

b Tick the state you find most metals in while at room temperature. Tick **one** box.

solid ☐   liquid ☐   gas ☐

c Draw a diagram to show how the atoms are arranged in a metal.

2 We can link the properties of metals to their structure.

Complete the following sentences by circling the correct answer.

a The melting and boiling points of metals are **high / low** because of strong bonds.

b Metals are **flexible / brittle** because the layers can slide over each other.

c All metals are good **conductors / insulators** because the electrons are free to move.

3 Copper is an example of a metal that is not very reactive. It is flexible and a good conductor.

Give **two** uses of copper linked to its properties.

It is used for _____ because it is unreactive.

It is used for _____ because it is a good conductor.

4 Aluminium is another metal. It is more reactive than iron, but we use it in our gardens for greenhouses and gardening equipment. It isn't weakened by corrosion like iron is (when pieces of iron oxide flake off).

Why are we able to use aluminium to make gardening products without them being weakened by corrosion?

_____

10.2 Alloys

1 Alloys are mixtures that are mostly metal.

Which of the following is an alloy? Tick **one** box.

A

B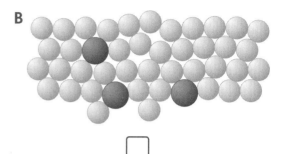

☐   ☐

2 Tick to show whether each statement about alloys is **true** or **false**.

	Statement	True	False
A	An alloy of a metal would be the pure element		
B	An alloy is a mixture		
C	An alloy changes the properties of a metal, for example, making a metal stronger or stopping corrosion		
D	Gold is often mixed in an alloy with metals like copper when producing jewellery to make it harder so it doesn't go out of shape		
E	Adding another substance to a metal can stop the layers sliding over each other as easily (making it less flexible)		

3 Steel is an alloy that is so useful that many countries have factories dedicated to producing it.

a Which metal is all steel made from? _____

b Which other element (a non-metal) is found in steel? _____

c Stainless steel is a type of steel.

It is stronger than some types of steel but it also resists corrosion.

Why does this property make it good for making cutlery from?

_____

10.3 Extracting metals

1 Name a metal that is unreactive and is usually found in the earth as a pure element (not joined to another element in a compound).

_____

2 Reactive metals need to be extracted from the rock they are found in.

  a What do we call a rock that contains a large amount of metal?

  _____

  b What do we call the process that removes the metal from the compounds found in these rocks?

  _____

3 Metals that are less reactive than carbon can be extracted by using carbon. Use the diagram to answer these questions.

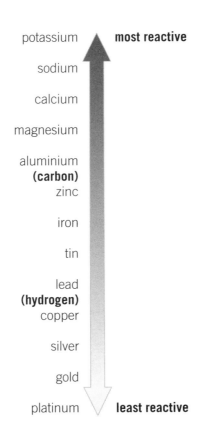

potassium **most reactive**
sodium
calcium
magnesium
aluminium
(carbon)
zinc
iron
tin
lead
(hydrogen)
copper
silver
gold
platinum **least reactive**

  a Name a metal that can be extracted using carbon. _____

  b Name a metal that **cannot** be extracted using carbon. _____

10.4 Recycling metals

1 Bauxite is the world's main source of aluminium. It is an aluminium ore.

What do we mean by an ore? _____

_____

2 Where would you find a metal ore?

_____

3 Metal ores can be quarried or mined depending on how deep they are found.

a Give **one** advantage to having a quarry near to a community.

_____

b Give **one** disadvantage to having a quarry near to a community.

_____

4 One of the advantages of using metals for goods is that they are easy to recycle.

a What is recycling?

_____

b List **two** reasons we should recycle as much metal as possible.

1 _____

2 _____

Now I know:	☹	😐	☺
The properties of metals and where they are found on the periodic table			
Some properties and uses of copper and aluminium			
What an alloy is			
Why an alloy would be used instead of using the pure metal			
How to determine which metals can be extracted by carbon, using the reactivity series			
Some of the benefits and drawbacks to having a quarry or mine near a community			
Why metals are recycled			

10.5 The reactivity series

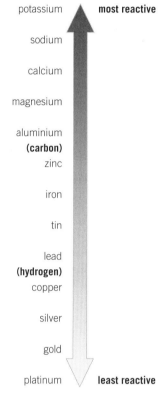

potassium — **most reactive**
sodium
calcium
magnesium
aluminium
(carbon)
zinc
iron
tin
lead
(hydrogen)
copper
silver
gold
platinum — **least reactive**

1   The reactivity series is a list of metals, plus hydrogen and carbon, that can be used to predict reactions.

Use the reactivity series to answer the questions below.

a   Name a metal less reactive than copper. _____

b   Which metal is more reactive – calcium or aluminium?

_____

2   During a displacement reaction, a more reactive metal takes the place of a less reactive metal.

The diagram below shows how iron displaces copper from copper compounds.

copper sulfate + iron ⟶ iron sulfate + copper

Complete the table to show if a displacement reaction occurs, and what products are made.

Chemicals mixed together	Will a displacement reaction occur?	Chemicals present at the end
Silver nitrate + gold		
Copper sulfate + zinc		
Zinc chloride + magnesium		

3   Circle the metals that will react with acid.

calcium   copper   iron   magnesium

10.6 Electrolysis

1   Ionic compounds are made of a metal and one or more non-metals.

Circle the ionic compounds.

Copper oxide   Methane (CH$_4$)   Nitrogen oxide

Carbon dioxide   Magnesium chloride   Aluminium oxide

2   When ions are free to move around (when they are dissolved or melted) they will conduct electricity.

Tick the correct name for the conducting sticks placed in the liquid during electrolysis.

Electrode ☐   Electrolyte ☐   Electrolysis ☐

3   The diagram shows the electrolysis of aluminium ore.

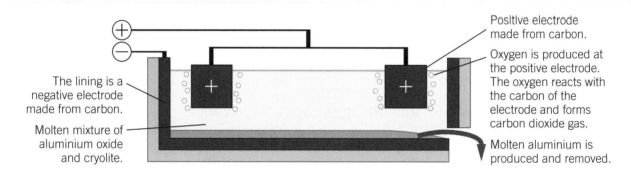

a   Why can't we just heat the ore with carbon to extract aluminium?

_____

b   Extraction of aluminium is expensive. Why is this?

_____

c   Look at the diagram of electrolysis of aluminium ore.
    Why might the positive electrode (anode) need replacing at regular intervals?

_____

10.7 Investigating electrolysis

1 The positive and negative electrodes have special names. What are they?

Positive electrode (+): _____   Negative electrode (–): _____

2 Draw **one** line to match each electrode to what is produced there.

Electrode   **What is produced at the electrode?**

| Positive (+) |

| Metal |

| Negative (–) |

| Non-metal |

3 a i What is made at the positive electrode when the dissolved ionic compound contains a halide (Group 7) ion?
Draw a circle around the correct answer.

   halogen gas   **hydrogen**   **metal**   **oxygen**

   ii What is made at the positive electrode when the solution **does not** contain halide ions?

   _____

   b i What is made at the negative electrode when the dissolved ionic compound contains a metal that is **more** reactive than hydrogen?
Draw a circle around the correct answer.

   halogen gas   **hydrogen**   **metal**   **oxygen**

   ii What is made at the negative electrode when the dissolved ionic compound contains a metal that is less reactive than hydrogen?

   _____

4 Complete the table to show the products of electrolysis at each electrode.

Electrolyte (and chemical formula)	Positive (+)	Negative (–)
Molten sodium chloride (NaCl)		
Sodium chloride solution (NaCl)		
Sulfuric acid (H_2SO_4)		

10.8 Sustainability

1 There is increasing pressure for us to develop and use products that are sustainable.

What does sustainable mean?

If something is sustainable it means we can use it but there will be enough

_____

2 Fossil fuels are an example of a finite resource.

What does finite mean?

There is only a certain

_____

3 Sort the following materials into ones that we should reduce, reuse, or recycle.
Some materials can be put into more than one box.

| food waste | empty drinks can | clothing | disposable nappies |
| empty glass jar | | plastic storage container | |

Reduce	Reuse	Recycle
_____	_____	_____
_____	_____	_____
_____	_____	_____

Now I know:	☹	😐	☺
What the reactivity series is			
How to use the reactivity series to predict displacement reactions			
What electrolysis is and which group of chemicals undergo electrolysis			
The scientific names of the positive and negative electrodes			
What is made at the electrodes during electrolysis			
What being sustainable means			
How reducing, reusing, and recycling can help us to be sustainable			

Component 3: Exam-style questions

1. Draw **one** line from each model to the state of matter that it represents.　　　**[2 marks]**

Model　　　　　　　　　　　　　　　　　　　State of matter

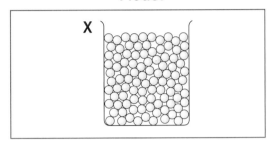

gas

liquid

solid

2. The table shows the temperature at which a substance undergoes some changes of state.

Temperature in °C	Change of state
−39	Solid to liquid
357	Liquid to gas

a　Which temperature is the melting point of the substance?　　　**[1 mark]**

....

b　The substance is made up of only one type of atom.

What is the name given to this type of substance?

Draw a ring around the correct answer.　　　**[1 mark]**

Compound　　　　　　　Element　　　　　　　Mixture

c   The substance is a metal.

What is one property of metals?

Tick (✓) **one** box.   [1 mark]

Do not conduct electricity   ☐

Conduct heat well   ☐

Weak bonds between atoms   ☐

3. This question is about metals.

Use the correct answer from each box to complete each sentence.   [2 marks]

a | an ore | granite | limestone |

A rock that contains enough metal to be economically worth extracting is called ....

b | alloy | compound | ore |

We sometimes add a substance to a metal to change its properties, for example, we add carbon to iron to make steel.

Steel is an example of an ....

4. a   Sodium reacts with a substance to form sodium chloride.

What is the other substance?   [1 mark]

....

b Sodium also reacts with hydrogen to form sodium hydride.

Sodium is a solid element. Hydrogen is a gas element. Sodium hydride is a compound.

Draw **one** line from the model to the substance that the model represents. **[2 marks]**

Model

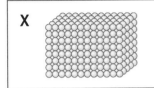

X

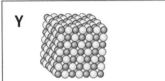

Y

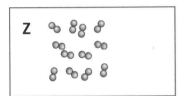

Z

Substance

Hydrogen

Sodium

Sodium hydride

c Sodium also reacts with oxygen.

Complete the word equation for the reaction between sodium and oxygen. **[1 mark]**

Sodium + oxygen → ....

5. The diagram shows part of the periodic table.

																	8
																	4
																	He
Group				relative atomic mass		1.0											helium
				chemical symbol		H					3	4	5	6	7		2
1	2			name		hydrogen											
				atomic (proton) number		1											
7	9										11	12	14	16	19	20	
Li	Be										B	C	N	O	F	Ne	
lithium	beryllium										boron	carbon	nitrogen	oxygen	fluorine	neon	
3	4										5	6	7	8	9	10	
23	24										27	28	31	32	35.5	40	
Na	Mg										Al	Si	P	S	Cl	Ar	
sodium	magnesium										aluminium	silicon	phosphorus	sulfur	chlorine	argon	
11	12										13	14	15	16	17	18	
39	40	45	48	51	52	55	56	59	59	63.5	65	70	73	75	79	80	84
K	Ca	Sc	Ti	V	Cr	Mn	Fe	Co	Ni	Cu	Zn	Ga	Ge	As	Se	Br	Kr
potassium	calcium	scandium	titanium	vanadium	chromium	manganese	iron	cobalt	nickel	copper	zinc	gallium	germanium	arsenic	selenium	bromine	krypton
19	20	21	22	23	24	25	26	27	28	29	30	31	32	33	34	35	36
85.5	88	89	91	93	96	(98)	101	103	106	108	112	115	119	122	128	127	131
Rb	Sr	Y	Zr	Nb	Mo	Tc	Ru	Rh	Pd	Ag	Cd	In	Sn	Sb	Te	I	Xe
rubidium	strontium	yttrium	zirconium	niobium	molybdenum	technetium	ruthenium	rhodium	palladium	silver	cadmium	indium	tin	antimony	tellurium	iodine	xenon
37	38	39	40	41	42	43	44	45	46	47	48	49	50	51	52	53	54
133	137	139	178.5	181	184	186	190	192	195	197	201	204	207	209	210	(210)	222
Cs	Ba	La	Hf	Ta	W	Re	Os	Ir	Pt	Au	Hg	Tl	Pb	Bi	Po	At	Rn
caesium	barium	lanthanum	hafnium	tantalum	tungsten	rhenium	osmium	iridium	platinum	gold	mercury	thallium	lead	bismuth	polonium	astatine	radon
55	56	57	72	73	74	75	76	77	78	79	80	81	82	83	84	85	86
(223)	(226)	(227)	(261)	(262)	(266)	(264)	(277)	(268)	(271)	(272)	(285)	(286)	(289)	(289)	(293)	(294)	(294)
Fr	Ra	Ac	Rf	Db	Sg	Bh	Hs	Mt	Ds	Rg	Cn	Nh	Fl	Mc	Lv	Ts	Og
francium	radium	actinium	rutherfordium	dubnium	seaborgium	bohrium	hassium	meitnerium	darmstadtium	roentgenium	copernicium	nihonium	flerovium	moscovium	livermorium	Tennessine	Oganesson
87	88	89	104	105	106	107	108	109	110	111	112	113	114	115	116	117	118

a What does each of the boxes in the periodic table show? [1 mark]

Tick (✓) **one** box.

An element ☐

A compound ☐

A mixture ☐

b On which side of the periodic table do you find the non-metals? [1 mark]

Tick (✓) **one** box.

Left ☐

Right ☐

c Which group contains the reactive non-metals (the halogens)? [1 mark]

....

d Which group contains the alkali metals? [1 mark]

....

6. Mixtures are different from compounds.

a Which of the following substances is a mixture?
Circle the correct answer. [1 mark]

magnesium chloride   **salt in water**   **carbon**

b Which method can you use to separate sand from water? [1 mark]

Tick (✓) **one** box.

Crystallisation ☐

Distillation ☐

Filtration ☐

7. The pigments in this sample of paint have been separated by chromatography.

Which **two** colours does the paint contain? [2 marks]

....

....

red   orange yellow   paint   pencil
                             sample   line

filter
paper

8. Polymers are long molecules made of many repeating units.

The diagram shows the structure of a polymer.

a   What is the name of the small molecule that makes up a polymer?   [1 mark]

....

b   Draw a circle around the repeating unit of the polymer.   [1 mark]

9. The diagram shows the reactivity series of different metals.

a   What is **one** metal that can be found as the metal itself
in the Earth?   [1 mark]

....

b   What is **one** metal that can be extracted using
carbon?   [1 mark]

....

c   It costs £8.40 to extract 1 kg of a metal from a rock.

The metal can be sold at a cost of £40 for 5 kg.

Is the rock an ore?   [2 marks]

....

....

d   We can recycle metal and use it again and again.

What is **one** advantage of recycling metals?   [1 mark]

....

01 All substances are made up of atoms.

Atoms themselves contain different types of sub-atomic particles.

01.1 Complete the table to show the charges of the sub-atomic particles. **[3 marks]**

Sub-atomic particle	Relative charge
Proton	
Electron	
	0

01.2 Magnesium can be represented as $^{24}_{12}Mg$.

How many protons does magnesium have? **[1 mark]**

_____

01.3 Nitrogen can be represented as $^{14}_{7}N$.

Draw the electronic structure for nitrogen. **[2 marks]**

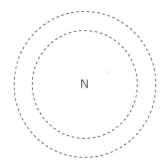

01.4 How many electrons are in the outermost shell of an atom from Group 2 in the periodic table? **[1 mark]**

_____

02 Complete the table by choosing the correct type of bonding for each of the statements.

Tick **one** column in each row. **[3 marks]**

Statement	Ionic	Covalent
Conducts electricity when dissolved in aqueous solution		
Has positive and negative ions		
Electrons in the outer shell are shared between atoms		

03 Zinc has an atomic number of 30 and a mass number of 65.

03.1 How many electrons does zinc have?   **[1 mark]**

_____

03.2 How many neutrons does zinc have?   **[1 mark]**

_____

04 Carbon can exist as diamond or graphite.

04.1 Draw **one** line from each property to the correct structure.   **[3 marks]**

Property	Structure
strong and hard	diamond
soft and slippery	graphite
does not conduct electricity	

04.2 Describe the structure of graphite.   **[3 marks]**

_____

_____

_____

04.3 Carbon atoms can exist as isotopes.

Two isotopes of carbon are carbon-12 and carbon-13.

The atomic symbol of carbon-12 is $^{12}_{6}C$.

How many protons does carbon-13 have? Tick **one** answer.   **[1 mark]**

6 ☐

7 ☐

12 ☐

13 ☐

05   Lithium is a Group 1 metal.

05.1 Give **one** property of Group 1 metals.   **[1 mark]**

_____

05.2 Lithium reacts with chlorine.

Complete the word equation for this reaction.   **[1 mark]**

lithium + chlorine ⟶ _____

05.3 Potassium is another Group 1 metal.

Explain why potassium is more reactive than lithium.   **[2 marks]**

_____

_____

_____

06   **Figure 1** shows the reactivity series for metals
         (with carbon and hydrogen included).

Figure 1

potassium	most reactive
sodium	
calcium	
magnesium	
aluminium	
(carbon)	
zinc	
iron	
tin	
lead	
(hydrogen)	
copper	
silver	
gold	
platinum	least reactive

06.1 The following reactants are placed in test tubes labelled A–D.

In which test tube will a displacement reaction occur?   **[1 mark]**

Tick **one** box.

A   Copper sulfate + magnesium   ☐

B   Copper chloride + silver   ☐

C   Magnesium sulfate + copper   ☐

D   Zinc nitrate + copper   ☐

06.2 Name the **two** products formed in the displacement
         reaction from question **06.1**.   **[2 marks]**

_____

_____

07   Bromine is a Group 7 non-metal element.

07.1   Complete the dot and cross diagram to show the covalent bond in a
bromine molecule.   **[1 mark]**

07.2   Magnesium is a group 2 metal element.

Bromine reacts with magnesium to form magnesium bromide.

Name the type of bonding in magnesium bromide.   **[1 mark]**

_____

07.3   What is one property you would expect magnesium bromide to have?

Tick **one** answer.   **[1 mark]**

Conducts electricity when solid ☐

Gas at room temperature ☐

Giant structure ☐

Low melting pint ☐

08   Ionic compounds can undergo electrolysis.

To undergo electrolysis, they must be molten or dissolved in solution.

08.1   Sodium chloride is an ionic compound.

Why does sodium chloride only undergo electrolysis when molten or in solution?

Tick **one** box.   **[1 mark]**

Atoms can move around in the liquid ☐

Ions move about in the liquid ☐

Molecules move around in the liquid ☐

Water molecules are present ☐

08.2 A student carries out the electrolysis of molten sodium chloride.

The electrolysis produces sodium metal and chlorine gas.

Draw **one** line from each product to the electrode that the substance is produced at. **[1 mark]**

Product	Electrode
Sodium metal	Anode (+)
Chlorine gas	Cathode (−)

08.3 The student collects some of the chlorine gas.

Describe a test the student should carry out to show that the gas is chlorine.

Include the result that would be observed. **[2 marks]**

_____

_____

09 Aluminium is found as aluminium oxide in its ores.

Electrolysis is used to extract aluminium from aluminium oxide.

09.1 Complete the word equation for the electrolysis of aluminium oxide. **[1 mark]**

aluminium oxide ⟶ _____ + _____

09.2 Aluminium oxide is mixed with cryolite before it undergoes electrolysis.

Give the purpose of mixing aluminium oxide with cryolite. **[1 mark]**

_____

09.3 In the electrolysis of aluminium oxide, the positive electrode is made out of carbon.

Explain why the positive carbon electrode needs to be replaced on a regular basis. **[2 marks]**

_____

_____

09.4 Aluminium metal can be recycled.

Give **one** advantage to recycling aluminium metal over extracting it from its ore. **[1 mark]**

_____

10   The table shows the melting point of three substances.

Substance	Melting point in °C
A	−114
B	801
C	79–94

10.1 Identify which substance is a small covalent molecule.   **[1 mark]**

_____

10.2 Identify which substance is a mixture.   **[1 mark]**

_____

10.3 One substance is sodium chloride.

Identify which substance is sodium chloride.   **[1 mark]**

_____

10.4 Sodium chloride can dissolve in water to make a solution.

A student dissolved 75 g of sodium chloride in 0.3 dm³ of water.

Calculate the concentration of the solution.

Use the formula:

$$\text{Concentration (g/dm}^3) = \frac{\text{mass of sodium (g)}}{\text{volume of water (dm}^3)}$$ **[2 marks]**

_____ g / dm³

11 Reactions of acids

Key words

acid   base   alkali   neutralisation   crystallisation   filtration   evaporation   salt

11.1 Neutralisation

1   We can recognise chemicals that are acids or alkalis based on their pH values.

Complete the table to show which range is alkali, acid, and neutral.

pH range	Group of chemicals
Less than 7	
Around 7	
More than 7	

2   Bases are chemicals that can react with an acid to neutralise it and produce a salt and water.

Which of the following chemicals are bases? Tick **three** boxes.

Carbon dioxide ☐   Magnesium oxide ☐   Sodium hydroxide ☐

Sodium chloride ☐   Water ☐   Calcium carbonate ☐

3   The reactions of metal compounds with acids are predictable:

   – Metal hydroxides and oxides react with acids to make → a salt + water

   – Metal carbonates react with acids to make → a salt + water + carbon dioxide

   – Sulfuric acid always makes sulfates

   – Hydrochloric acid always makes chlorides

Complete the reactions below with the names of the products.

a Potassium hydroxide +   Sulfuric acid   → _____ + _____

b Magnesium oxide   + Hydrochloric acid → _____ + _____

c Calcium carbonate   + Hydrochloric acid → _____ + _____ + _____

d Sodium hydroxide   +   Sulfuric acid   → _____ + _____

e Copper carbonate   +   Sulfuric acid   → _____ + _____ + _____

4   When a neutralisation reaction is finished, the salt (chemical) produced is dissolved in water.

Name the separation technique used to get the dry salt from the salt solution.

_____

11.2 Metals and acids

1 Many metals react with acid to produce a gas.

   a   What gas is produced? _____

   b   Describe how we could test the gas to prove what it is.

   _____

2 The products made when a metal and an acid react will always include
a gas and a metal salt.

The name of the salt depends on the type of acid used.

Sulfuric acid always makes sulfates and hydrochloric acid makes chlorides.

Complete the reactions below with the names of the products: a salt and a gas each time.

   a Magnesium +   Sulfuric acid   → _____ + _____

   b   Zinc   + Hydrochloric acid → _____ + _____

   c Magnesium + Hydrochloric acid → _____ + _____

   d   Iron   +   Sulfuric acid   → _____ + _____

3 Name a metal (low in the reactivity series) that is unreactive with acid. _____

11.3 Investigating acids and carbonates

1 Metal carbonates react with acids to make a salt, water, and a gas.

   a   Name this type of reaction. _____

   b   Name the gas produced. _____

   c   How do you test for this gas? _____

2 A group of students carried out a reaction between sulfuric acid and copper carbonate.
They kept adding the copper carbonate to some sulfuric acid until the acid had all reacted.
After it had finished reacting, they used universal indicator paper to test the pH.

   a   How would they see that all the acid had reacted?

   _____

   b   Would the pH of the solution be higher or lower than the pH of the original acid?
       Tick **one** box.

   higher ☐   lower ☐

c   At the end of the reaction, there was some leftover copper carbonate (solid) at the bottom of the beaker of copper sulfate solution.

The students now want to get dry copper sulfate crystals from the solution in their beaker. Complete the table to show the three separation techniques needed to get this dry salt.

Apparatus			
What the students are doing	Removing the insoluble copper carbonate from the liquid		
The name of the technique			

Now I know:	☹	😐	☺
What acids, bases, and alkalis are			
That neutralisation reactions involve an acid being neutralised or used up and water being made			
The products (chemicals made) of neutralisation reactions			
The products (chemicals made) of the reaction between a metal and acid			
How to collect the dry product (chemical made) of a neutralisation reaction			

Key words

pH   ions   balanced symbol equation   state symbols

11.4 The pH scale

1   For each pH below, write whether it is acid, alkali, or neutral, and give the colour it turns in universal indicator.

   a   1:   _____   _____

   b   7:   _____   _____

   c   14:   _____   _____

2   All acids can dissolve in water.

   a   Name the particle made when an acid dissolves in water. _____

   b   Write the formula for this particle. _____

3   Alkalis are soluble bases (bases that dissolve in water).

   a   Name the particle made when an alkali dissolves in water. _____

   b   Write the formula for this particle. _____

4   When an acid and an alkali react they always produce water.
    We call this a neutralisation reaction.

   a   What will the pH be at the end of a neutralisation reaction? _____

   b   We can write the word equation for neutralisation as: Hydrogen ions + hydroxide ions → water

       Write the symbol equation for this reaction. Include state symbols.

       _____ (___)   +   _____ (___)   →   _____ (___)

5   Draw lines to form two correct statements about pH.

| A solution with a pH > 7 | is an acid | because there are many hydrogen ions in the solution. |
| A solution with a pH < 7 | is an alkali | because there are many hydroxide ions in the solution. |

11.5 Balanced symbol equations

1 Write the chemical formula for each of the substances below.

Take care with the size of the numbers in the formulae.

| Zn | CO_2 | H_2O | Cl_2 | H_2SO_4 | O_2 | HCl | $CuCO_3$ |

Compound	Formula
Chlorine	
Oxygen	
Water	
Copper carbonate	

Compound	Formula
Zinc	
Hydrochloric acid	
Sulfuric acid	
Carbon dioxide	

2 The same number of atoms of each element must be present at the start and end of a chemical reaction.

Add numbers to the boxes to make each equation balance.

a ☐ $HCl + Mg \rightarrow MgCl_2 + H_2$

c $2H_2 + O_2 \rightarrow$ ☐ H_2O

b $2CO + O_2 \rightarrow$ ☐ CO_2

d ☐ $Mg + O_2 \rightarrow$ ☐ MgO

3 State symbols are very important because they tell us if a chemical is solid (s), liquid (l), gas (g), or dissolved in a solution (aq).

Add state symbols to the equations below.

a $CuCO_3(s)$ + $2HCl(\underline{\quad})$ $\rightarrow$ $CuCl_2(aq)$ + $CO_2(\underline{\quad})$ + $H_2O(\underline{\quad})$

b $Mg(\underline{\quad})$ + $H_2SO_4(\underline{\quad})$ $\rightarrow$ $MgSO_4(aq)$ + $H_2(\underline{\quad})$

c $NaOH(\underline{\quad})$ + $HCl(\underline{\quad})$ $\rightarrow$ $NaCl(\underline{\quad})$ + $H_2O(\underline{\quad})$

Now I know:	☹	😐	☺
The pH values for acids, alkalis, and neutral solutions			
What happens to the hydrogen and hydroxide ions in a neutralisation reaction			
How to balance a symbol equation			
What state symbols mean and how to add them to the equation for a chemical reaction			

12 Energy and rate of reaction

Key words

energy transfer   rate of reaction   collision   catalyst

12.1 Energy transfers

1   When chemical or physical changes take place, energy is transferred between the system (the substances that are reacting or changing) and the surroundings.

   a   When energy is transferred from the chemicals to the surroundings, what happens to the temperature of the surroundings? Tick the correct option.

   Increases ☐   Decreases ☐

   b   When energy is transferred from the surroundings to the chemicals, what happens to the temperature of the surroundings? Tick the correct option.

   Increases ☐   Decreases ☐

2   Look at the chemical reactions below. Where is the energy transferred?

Reactants	Temperature change	Transfer to the surroundings OR to the system?
Magnesium + oxygen	Up	
Citric acid + sodium hydrogen carbonate	Down	
Methane (natural gas) + oxygen	Up	
Ammonium chloride + water	Down	

12.2 Rate of reaction

1   Magnesium ribbon reacts with warm acid and cold acid.

   a   Will the reaction with cold acid be faster or slower than with warm acid?

   _____

   b   Circle the correct words to complete the sentence.

   In the warm acid, the particles are moving **faster** / **slower**, so collisions are **less** / **more** likely to occur.

2 Concentrated hydrochloric acid reacts faster than dilute hydrochloric acid.

Explain why the concentrated acid reacts faster. Include the term **collisions** in your answer.

Because there are _____ particles of _____

_____

3 a Powdered magnesium reacts faster than magnesium ribbon with the same acid.

Which particle diagram is which?

Powdered magnesium _____

Magnesium ribbon _____

X   Y

⬤ magnesium particle   ◯ acid particle

b Explain why powdered magnesium reacts faster. Refer to **collisions** in your answer.

Because the surface area is _____

_____

4 A catalyst can change the rate of a chemical reaction.

Complete the table to show which statements about catalysts are true and which are false.

Statement	True or false?
A catalyst will slow down the rate of a chemical reaction	
The catalyst is used up in the chemical reaction	
Using a catalyst lowers the amount of energy that the particles need to collide with for a reaction to happen	

12.3 Monitoring rate of reaction

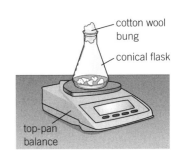

cotton wool bung

conical flask

top-pan balance

1   One way to measure the rate of reaction is to measure the mass of a reaction mixture.

a   Tick the type of reaction you can measure with this technique.

A neutralisation reaction between an acid and an alkali ☐

A reaction when a solid reacts to produce a gas ☐

A reaction that makes a solid from a solution (precipitate) ☐

b   Would you expect the mass to go up or down?

Up ☐   Down ☐

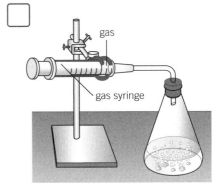

gas

gas syringe

2   Another way of measuring the rate of reaction is to measure how much gas is produced in a set amount of time.

Tick the graph that shows the reaction between calcium carbonate and hydrochloric acid.

A ☐

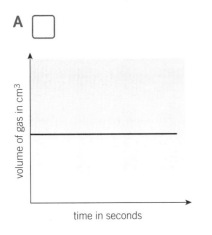

time in seconds

B ☐

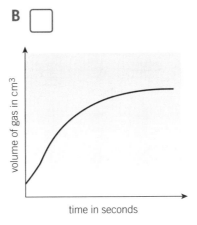

time in seconds

C ☐

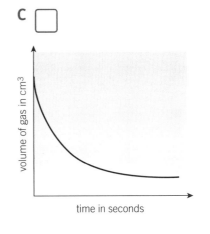

time in seconds

Now I know:	😞	😐	😊
How to classify reactions as transferring energy to the surroundings or to the system (from the surroundings) by measuring the reaction temperature			
How increasing temperature, concentration, and surface area increase the rate of reaction (using collision theory)			
What a catalyst does			
How rate of reaction is calculated by measuring decreases in mass, volume of gases produced, or time for a solution to become opaque (when you can't see a cross through it)			

exothermic   endothermic   activation energy   reaction profile

12.4 Reaction profiles

1   Draw **one** line from each type of reaction to its description and to its reaction profile.

Type of reaction	Description	Reaction profile

Endothermic

Transfers energy to the surroundings so there is a temperature increase

Exothermic

Transfers energy from the surroundings so there is a temperature decrease

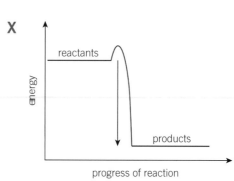

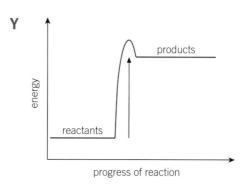

2   a   What term do we use for the minimum amount of energy needed by particles when they collide for a reaction to occur?

_____

b   Which letter represents this on the reaction profile? _____

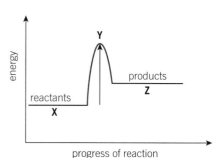

3 a How does a catalyst change the rate of a reaction?

_____

b What effect would a catalyst have on the activation energy?

_____

12.5 Measuring the rate of a reaction

1 Tick the correct formula for calculating the rate of a reaction.

A mean rate of reaction = $\dfrac{\text{amount of reactant used or product made}}{\text{time}}$ ☐

B mean rate of reaction = $\dfrac{\text{time}}{\text{amount of reactant used or product made}}$ ☐

C mean rate of reaction = (amount of reactant used or product made) × time ☐

2 Tick **two** units from the list below that can be used to measure the rate of a reaction.

m/s ☐ cm^3 ☐ cm^3/s ☐

gs ☐   g/s ☐ s/cm^3 ☐

3 A graph can be used to work out the rate of reaction. This graph shows reaction rates at three different temperatures.

a Which of the lines on the graph shows the fastest rate of reaction? _____

b Why do the lines on the graph all level off at the same point?

_____

volume of gas produced in cm^3 (vertical axis)

X, Y, Z (curves)

time in seconds (horizontal axis)

4 Calcium carbonate lumps were reacted with excess hydrochloric acid. During the reaction, 10 g of calcium carbonate reacted in 5 seconds.

What was the mean rate of the reaction? Tick **one** box.

5 g/s ☐   2 g/s ☐   0.5 g/s ☐

$5\ cm^3/s$ ☐ $2\ cm^3/s$ ☐ $0.5\ cm^3/s$ ☐

12.6 Investigating rate of a reaction

1 Name **two** factors that could affect the rate of a reaction, apart from concentration.

1 _____ 2 _____

2 A student wanted to investigate the effect of concentration on rate of reaction for calcium carbonate and hydrochloric acid.

Which of the following variables would they change? Tick **one** box.

A The temperature of the acid (0 °C, 20 °C, 50 °C) ☐

B The concentration of the acid (10 g/dm³, 20 g/dm³, 40 g/dm³) ☐

C The size of the calcium carbonate lumps (powder, small pieces, large pieces) ☐

3 An experiment was carried out using two different concentrations of hydrochloric acid and calcium metal. The volume of gas produced was recorded at regular intervals.

The graph shows the results from this experiment.

a At point **X**, which of the reactions would have the fastest rate of reaction? Circle the correct answer.

80 g/dm³ acid   **40 g/dm³ acid**

b Tick the correct answer for the reaction at point **Y**.

The reaction rate of the 80 g/dm³ acid is fastest. ☐

The reaction rate of the 40 g/dm³ acid is fastest. ☐

Both reactions have finished (so the rate would be zero). ☐

Now I know:	☹	😐	☺
The energy changes involved in exothermic and endothermic reactions			
What the activation energy is			
How a catalyst works by lowering the activation energy			
How the rate of reaction is calculated			
How the rate of a reaction is investigated in the laboratory			

13 Fuels and the atmosphere

Key words

atmosphere   photosynthesis   crude oil   fractional distillation   fraction   complete
combustion   incomplete combustion   hydrocarbon   acid rain
greenhouse gases   global climate change

13.1 Development of the atmosphere

1 The atmosphere of the Earth 3 billion years ago was very different to our current atmosphere.
  There was no oxygen and lots of carbon dioxide.

  a Name the process used by plants which uses carbon dioxide and releases oxygen.

  _____

  b Give another process that removed carbon dioxide from the atmosphere.

  _____

2 Put the following stages in the correct order to show the evolution of the Earth's atmosphere.

W	X	Y	Z
Early life took carbon dioxide from the atmosphere and released oxygen.	The level of carbon dioxide fell and the level of oxygen increased.	Volcanic eruptions produced gases and water vapour, which formed the first atmosphere.	The Earth cooled and the water vapour condensed.

Correct order: ☐ ☐ ☐ ☐

3 The diagram below shows the proportion of gases that make up the current atmosphere. The
  most common gases in the atmosphere are oxygen, nitrogen, argon, and carbon dioxide.

  Name the gases shown in the diagram.

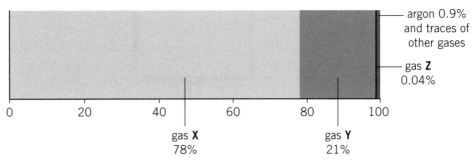

Gas	Name of gas
X	
Y	
Z	

argon 0.9% and traces of other gases

gas Z 0.04%

gas X 78%

gas Y 21%

13.2 Crude oil

1 Where do we find crude oil?

_____

2 What is crude oil made from?

_____

3 Crude oil is a mixture of chemicals.

Some of them have high boiling points and some have low boiling points.

a What is the name of the process that is used to separate these chemicals?

_____

b Add an arrow next to the diagram below to show how the temperature increases.

c Put the fuels below in the correct boxes of the diagram to show where these fractions (chemicals) would be taken out of the separation process.

> **Petroleum gases and petrol** (relatively low boiling points)
>
> **Diesel and tar** (high boiling points)

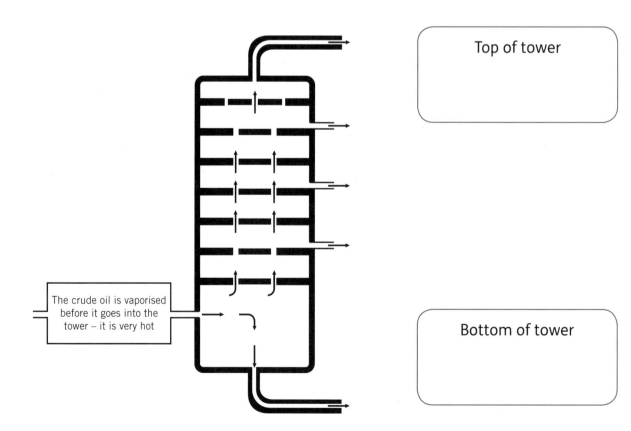

Top of tower

The crude oil is vaporised before it goes into the tower – it is very hot

Bottom of tower

13.3 Fuels and combustion

1 Fuels separated from crude oil are called fossil fuels. They are hydrocarbons.

Why are they called hydrocarbons?

_____

2 Fuel requires oxygen to burn.

a Name the two products (what is made) of the complete combustion of methane (CH_4).

1 _____ 2 _____

b Name the dangerous gas produced by the incomplete combustion of methane.

_____

3 Complete the sentence to show you can test the gas produced during complete combustion.

We could test the gas by bubbling it through limewater. It should turn _____

if _____ is present.

4 One example of incomplete combustion is burning natural gas
(methane) with an orange flame, using a Bunsen burner.

What is the black substance left on glassware when you hold it over an orange flame?

_____

5 Petrol is a hydrocarbon fossil fuel that is separated from crude oil.

Complete the word equation for the complete combustion of petrol.

Petrol + oxygen → _____ + _____

13.4 Air pollution

1   Acid rain can be harmful to living organisms.

Name the two chemicals that can cause acid rain.

1 _____   2 _____

2   What effect does acid rain have on rocks and buildings made of marble and limestone?

Acid rain reacts chemically with marble and limestone and causes _____

_____

3   Any combustion reaction can be dangerous if there is not enough oxygen for complete combustion to occur.

   a   What gas is made by incomplete combustion of a fuel? _____

   b   Why would this be dangerous to people nearby?

_____

4   Cars and machines that burn fossil fuels can release solid soot particles into the atmosphere.

The diagram shows these particles blocking sunlight from entering our atmosphere.

This reduces the total amount of light that reaches the surface of the Earth.

Name this global effect. _____

13.5 Climate change

1   The diagram shows how energy from the Sun can be trapped in the atmosphere by some of the gases it contains.

This causes the Earth to be warmer than it would be without the atmosphere.

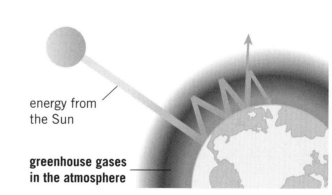

energy from
the Sun

greenhouse gases
in the atmosphere

   a   What is the name for this trapping of energy by the atmosphere?

_____

b The two main gases that cause this heating are carbon dioxide and methane.

Name the main source of each gas.

Carbon dioxide: _____

Methane: _____

2 Carbon dioxide levels are rising because of human activity.

How are the activities below increasing the amount of carbon dioxide in the atmosphere?

a Burning more fossil fuels in cars and power stations:

_____

b Cutting down huge areas of forest:

_____

3 Scientists are certain that the temperature of the Earth is being affected by human activity.

Name **two** possible effects of global climate change.

1 _____

2 _____

Now I know:	☹	😐	☺
How the atmosphere of the Earth evolved over time			
How photosynthesis has increased the level of oxygen in the atmosphere			
The names of the most common gases in the atmosphere			
What crude oil is and where it can be found			
How crude oil can be separated into different chemicals			
The products of complete and incomplete combustion			
How gases made during the combustion of fossil fuels can cause pollution			
What the greenhouse effect is and how it could lead to global climate change			

13.6 Cracking

1 Long-chain hydrocarbons can be split to make more useful short-chain molecules.

   What is the name of the process that causes them to split? _____

2 Splitting these long-chain hydrocarbons produces two types of molecules.

   These are **alkanes** (with single bonds) and **alkenes** (with carbon to carbon double bonds).

   Complete the table to name the chemicals shown and determine if they are alkanes or alkenes.

Diagram	Alkane or alkene?	Name
H—C—C—C=C (with H's)		But_____
H—C—C—H (with H's)		Eth_____
H—C—C—C—C—C—H (with H's)		Pent_____
C=C (with H's)		Eth_____

3 Some students tested four different chemicals with bromine water.

   Complete the table to show if each chemical is an alkane or an alkene.

Colour after adding bromine water and shaking	Alkane or alkene?
Orange	
Colourless	
Almost colourless	
Orange/brown	

13.7 Carbon footprint

1 Which gas are we referring to when we talk about the carbon footprint? _____

2 There are many ways that we can reduce our carbon footprint.

    a   Circle the activities that increase your carbon footprint.

       Cutting down trees   **Walking instead of driving**   **Planting trees**

          Using electricity made from burning coal or gas   **Flying in an aeroplane**

    b   How can each activity below reduce your carbon footprint?

        1.   Walking to work instead of driving:

        _____

        _____

        2.   Cutting down on how much meat you eat:

        _____

        _____

        3.   Recycling:

        _____

        _____

        4.   Switching to solar and wind power:

        _____

        _____

3 One suggested way of reducing carbon emissions is to capture the carbon dioxide produced and store it below ground.

Give **one** reason why this method is not currently being used in power stations across the world.

_____

Now I know:	☹	😐	☺
How long-chain alkanes can be split into useful shorter chains by cracking			
The structures of alkanes and alkenes			
How to test for an alkene			
What a carbon footprint is and how it might be reduced			

14 Water for drinking

Key words

potable water   dissolved solids   sterilised   distillation   pure water   water treatment

14.1 Drinking water

1   We need to treat water to make it safe to drink. We call this potable water.

Complete the table to show the correct order for the stages of water treatment.

What is happening	Number of stage (1–5)
The water is left so that the sand and soil settle at the bottom	
Aluminium sulfate and lime are added to make the small particles stick together and drop to the bottom	
Any harmful microbes that may be left are killed using chlorine, ozone, or UV light	
Water is screened to remove large objects like twigs	1
The water is checked to make sure it is ready to be used in homes and factories	

2   Another source of drinking water is distillation.

a   Use the words below to label the distillation equipment.

Thermometer
Drinking water
Undrinkable water
Cold water in
Water out
Condenser

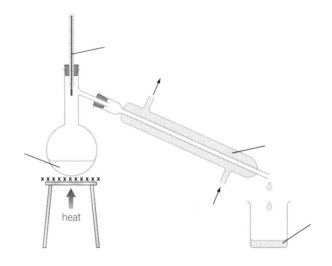

heat

b Distillation is a very expensive way of making drinking water.

What part of the process makes it so expensive?

_____

14.2 Investigating water

1 The diagram shows the apparatus needed to investigate the amount of dissolved solids in different samples of water.

a Give the correct order for the stages of the investigation.

Stage	Instructions to student
A	Allow the equipment to cool down.
B	Add 50 cm³ of the water sample to the beaker.
C	Measure the mass of the dry beaker with remaining solids.
D	Record the mass of a clean empty beaker.
E	Calculate the mass of dissolved solids: mass of solid = mass of beaker at the end – mass of beaker at the start
F	Set up the equipment as shown in the diagram and heat until the water has boiled away.

Correct order: D ☐ ☐ ☐ ☐ ☐

b The graph shows the mean mass of dissolved solids found in samples X, Y, and Z.

Which water sample was pure water?

_____

2 Water with dissolved solids can have a different pH.

What should the pH of pure water be?

_____

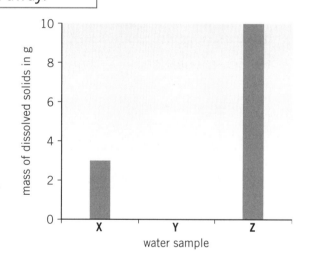

Now I know:	☹	😐	☺
What is meant by potable water			
The stages of treating water to make it potable			
How to distil undrinkable water to make potable water			
How to investigate the amount of dissolved solids in different water samples			

14.3 Waste water treatment

1   Sewage must be treated before the water can be used again or discharged into a river.

Why can't we put the raw sewage straight into a river without treating it?

It would be dangerous to our health because _____

_____

2   The table below shows the stages of treating water in a sewage treatment works, before the clean water is pumped back into the river.

Complete the table, describing what is happening at each stage.

Name of stage	What happens here?
Screening	
Sedimentation	
Aerobic digestion	

3   Methane gas is produced in the treatment of sewage.

a   What can methane gas be used for?

_____

b   Sewage sludge is also produced. What can sewage sludge be used for?

_____

Now I know:	☹	😐	☺
Why sewage needs to be treated before the water can be used			
How sewage is treated			
How sludge from the sewage treatment process can be used			

Component 4: Exam-style questions

1. The chart below shows the composition of the atmosphere today.

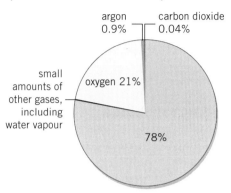

argon
0.9%

carbon dioxide
0.04%

small
amounts of
other gases,
including
water vapour

oxygen 21%

78%

a Which gas makes up 78% of the atmosphere today? **[1 mark]**

....

b The volume of oxygen in the early atmosphere was much lower.
Since life began, the volume of oxygen has increased.
Which process caused the increase in the volume of oxygen in the atmosphere? **[1 mark]**

Tick (✓) **one** box.

Combustion ☐

Decay ☐

Photosynthesis ☐

Respiration ☐

c Human activities are increasing the volume of greenhouse gases in the atmosphere.

Which of these gases are greenhouse gases? **[2 marks]**

Tick (✓) **two** boxes.

Methane ☐

Nitrogen ☐

Oxygen ☐

Sulfur dioxide ☐

d What is one human activity that has caused the increase
in this greenhouse gas in the atmosphere? **[1 mark]**

....

e Increases in greenhouse gases in the atmosphere lead to
global climate change.
What is one possible effect of global climate change? **[1 mark]**

....

2. Sherbet is made from citric acid and sodium hydrogen carbonate.
   When you eat sherbet, it makes your mouth feel cooler.

   Tick (✓) the correct ending to the sentence.   **[1 mark]**

   The chemical change in sherbet is...

   ... an energy transfer **to the surroundings.** ☐

   ... an energy transfer **from the surroundings.** ☐

3. Some countries don't have fresh water like rivers to use as a source
   of drinking water. Instead they must make drinking water from salt water.

   What is the name of the process used to remove the salt from sea water?   **[1 mark]**

   Tick (✓) **one** box.

   Boiling   ☐

   Distillation   ☐

   Evaporation   ☐

   Filtration   ☐

4. Crude oil is a mixture of chemicals that can be used as fuels.

   a   What is the technique used to separate crude oil?   **[1 mark]**

       Tick (✓) **one** box.

       Chromatography   ☐

       Crystallisation   ☐

       Filtration   ☐

       Fractional distillation ☐

   b   One chemical that is separate from crude oil is methane.
       Methane is used as a fuel in a process called combustion.

       Complete the word equation for the complete combustion of methane.   **[1 mark]**

       Use the correct words from the box.

       | carbon dioxide   nitrogen   oxygen |

       methane + ... → .... + water

c Methane can also undergo incomplete combustion.

What is **one** substance produced when a fuel undergoes
incomplete combustion?   [1 mark]

....

d Some fuels from crude oil can also have sulfur in them.
When the sulfur burns, this forms sulfur dioxide, which is released
into the atmosphere. Sulfur dioxide is an air pollutant.

What can the sulfur dioxide released into the atmosphere cause?   [1 mark]

Tick (✓) **one** box.

Acid rain   ☐

Global dimming   ☐

Global warming   ☐

5. A student reacts potassium carbonate with sulfuric acid. A gas is produced.

a What is the name of gas produced?   [1 mark]

Tick (✓) **one** box.

Carbon dioxide   ☐

Hydrogen   ☐

Oxygen   ☐

b The student bubbles the gas through limewater.
Use the words from the box to complete the sentence.   [1 mark]

┌───┐
│   clear   cloudy   colourful   │
└───┘

Limewater is ....

When the gas is bubbled through the limewater, it turns ....

c A salt is also formed when metal carbonates react with acid.
What is the name of the salt produced by this reaction?

Potassium ....   [1 mark]

d What type of reaction is this?

Tick (✓) **one** box.   [1 mark]

Combustion ☐

Neutralisation ☐

Oxidation ☐

6. Most drinking water in the UK comes from lakes, rivers, or in the ground.

   This water has to be treated before it is safe to drink.

   Draw **one** line from each process to the correct description for the process.   [2 marks]

Process	Description
	Kill any microbes in the water.
Flltratlon	
	Make pH 7
Sterilisation	
	Remove solids from the water

7. A student reacts calcium metal with hydrochloric acid in a test tube.

   a Circle the correct word from the box to complete the word equation for this reaction.

   chlorine

   Calcium + hydrochloric acid → calcium   chloride   + hydrogen   [1 mark]

   hydrochloric

   b The student notices that the test tube got warmer during the reaction.
   Choose the correct words from the boxes to complete the sentences.   [2 marks]

   increased   decreased

   During the reaction, the temperature of the surroundings ....

   to   from

   This means that energy was transferred .... the surroundings.

c   The student wants to collect the salt that was produced during the reaction.

The student knows they should use three steps to separate the salt from the mixture: crystallisation, evaporation, and filtration.

Put the three processes in the correct order to separate the salt from the solution.

The first one has been done for you.   **[1 mark]**

Process 1   **Process 2**   **Process 3**

| filtration | → | | → | |

8. A student investigated the rate of reaction of calcium with sulfuric acid at three different temperatures.

The student measured how much gas they collected in 5 minutes at each temperature.

The graph shows the student's results.

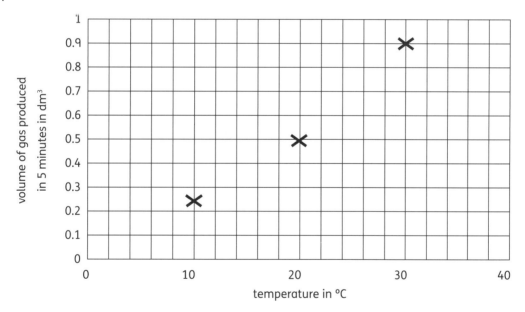

a   At which temperature was the rate of reaction fastest? .... **[1 mark]**

b   The gas collected is hydrogen gas.

Which method can be used to show the gas is hydrogen.   **[1 mark]**

Tick (✓) **one** answer.

Bubble gas through limewater   ☐

Damp blue litmus paper   ☐

Lit splint   ☐

c   What results from the test would you expect if the gas was hydrogen.   **[1 mark]**

....

9. A student set up two test tubes.

Test tube A had a piece of magnesium ribbon.

Test tube B has some powdered magnesium.

Both test tubes had the same mass of magnesium.

The student added the same volume of sulfuric acid to each test tube.

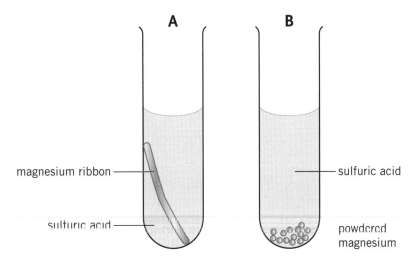

a Which test tube had the fastest rate of reaction?

.... [1 mark]

b What is one other way the rate of reaction could be increased?

Tick (✓) **one** box. [1 mark]

Decrease the concentration of sulfuric acid ☐

Decrease the temperature of sulfuric acid ☐

Increase the concentration of sulfuric acid ☐

01 Sewage is waste water from homes and industry.
It is taken away in separate drains to a treatment plant.

01.1 Draw **one** line from each water treatment process to its correct description. **[2 marks]**

Process		Description

Process
Screening

| Sedimentation |

| Aerobic digestion |

Description
Microbes break down organic matter in the presence of oxygen.
Grit and dirt allowed to settle out.
Large solids are removed.

01.2 Treated sewage sludge can be broken down by anaerobic microbes to make it safe to dispose of.

Which of these would you **not** expect to find in an anaerobic digester? **[1 mark]**

Tick **one** box.

Bacteria ☐

Methane ☐

Oxygen ☐

02 Potassium oxide is placed in a test tube with water and shaken.

Universal indicator is added. The pH of the solution formed is 14.

02.1 What colour would the universal indicator be? **[1 mark]**

_____

02.2 The potassium oxide solution is neutralised by adding hydrochloric acid.

What compound, other than water, is formed in this neutralisation reaction? **[1 mark]**

Tick **one** box.

Potassium chloride ☐

Potassium hydroxide ☐

Potassium oxide ☐

Potassium sulfate ☐

03 Carbon dioxide and methane are greenhouse gases.

Some human activities increase the amounts of carbon dioxide and methane in the atmosphere.

03.1 Give **one** human activity that increases the amount of carbon dioxide in the atmosphere.　　　　　　　　　　　　　　**[1 mark]**

_____

03.2 Most scientists believe that increasing greenhouse gases will result in global climate change.

Describe one effect global climate change could have.　　**[2 marks]**

_____

_____

_____

03.3 People can make lifestyle changes to reduce their carbon footprint.

Describe what a carbon footprint is.　　　　　　　　　　**[1 mark]**

_____

_____

04 When crude oil is separated, we end up with lots of long-chained alkanes, which are not as useful as shorter-chained alkanes.

04.1 Name the process used to break up these long-chained chemicals to get shorter useful ones.　　　　　　　　　　　　**[1 mark]**

_____

04.2 Alkanes are produced in this reaction.

Name the other type of hydrocarbon that will be produced.　　**[1 mark]**

_____

04.3 A student collects two samples of hydrocarbon, produced as a result of this process.

The student adds bromine water.

Complete the table to show what is in each test tube.　　　**[2 marks]**

Test tube	What happened with bromine water	What type of hydrocarbon must be in the test tube?
A	No change	
B	Bromine water lost its colour	

05 The pH of a solution is determined by the number of H^+ and OH^- ions in it.

Draw **one** line from each ion to its correct description. **[1 mark]**

Ion	Description

H⁺ → Lots of these ions makes the solution alkaline.

OH⁻ → Lots of these ions makes the solution acidic.

06 The table shows the pH of three different substances, W, X, and Y.

06.1 For each substance, identify whether it is an acid, an alkali, or neutral. **[3 marks]**

Substance	pH	Circle **one** answer for each row.		
W	2	acid	alkali	neutral
X	12	acid	alkali	neutral
Y	7	acid	alkali	neutral

06.2 Substance Z is tested with some universal indicator. The universal indicator turns red.

Is substance Z an acid, alkali, or neutral substance? **[1 mark]**

_____

07 Sodium reacts with hydrochloric acid to form a salt and hydrogen gas.

07.1 Name the salt produced. **[1 mark]**

_____

07.2 What type of reaction is this?

Tick **one** box. **[1 mark]**

Combustion ☐

Endothermic ☐

Neutralisation ☐

Oxidation ☐

07.3 The balanced symbol equation for this reaction is shown below.

Complete the balanced symbol equation by giving the missing state symbol. **[1 mark]**

$2Na(s) + 2HCl(aq) \rightarrow 2NaCl(aq) + H_2(\underline{\quad\quad})$

07.4 Sodium can also react with sulfuric acid.

Balance the symbol equation for the reaction of sodium and sulfuric acid. **[1 mark]**

_____ Na + H$_2$SO$_4$ → Na$_2$SO$_4$ + H$_2$

08 Potable water is water that is clean and safe to drink.

Some countries need to get potable water from sea water by a process called desalination.

08.1 Name the chemical that is removed from the water by this process. **[1 mark]**

_____

08.2 Desalination of water is very energy intensive.

We only use desalination when there is no other source of water that can be used.

Suggest **one** reason why. **[1 mark]**

_____

09 A student carried out an investigation to measure the effects of concentration of acid on the rate of reaction.
They plotted their results in the graph shown.

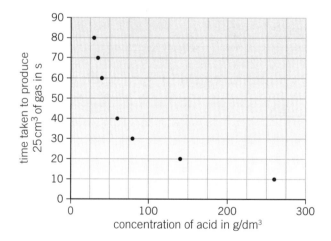

09.1 Complete the sentence to describe how concentration affects the rate of reaction. **[2 marks]**

As the concentration of the acid increases, the time taken to produce 25 cm^3 of gas _____.

This means that the rate of reaction is _____.

09.2 The student reacted the acid with copper oxide. The salt formed was copper sulfate.
Name the acid the student used in their reaction. **[1 mark]**

_____

09.3 The student investigated temperature changes during the chemical reaction.

What is the reading on this thermometer? **[1 mark]**

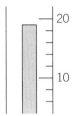

The temperature is _____ °C

09.4 The student noticed that the temperature increased during the reaction.

What type of reaction was it? **[1 mark]**

Tick **one** box.

Endothermic ☐

Exothermic ☐

09.5 Which of the following diagrams would describe the energy change for the chemical reaction? **[1 mark]**

Tick **one** box.

A

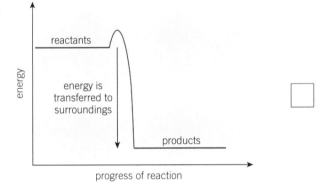

☐

B

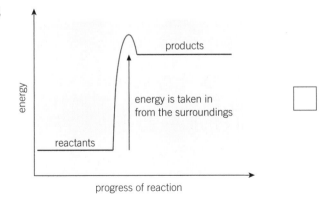

☐

15 Energy

Key words

energy store   energy transfer   chemical   kinetic   gravitational potential
thermal   elastic (strain)   conservation of energy   renewable   non-renewable
friction   conductor   insulator   thermal conductivity

15.1 Changes in energy stores

1   Name **three** examples of energy stores.

1 _____

2 _____

3 _____

2   Energy is transferred between different stores.

Complete the table to show the energy stores at the start and end of each energy transfer.

	Energy transfer	Energy store at start		Energy store at end
a	A catapult being released	Elastic	→	
b	A car braking		→	Thermal
c	Fuel burning		→	Thermal
d	A skydiver falling		→	Kinetic
e	Stretching a rubber band	Kinetic	→	

3   There are different ways (pathways) that energy can be transferred between energy stores.

Choose the correct pathway for each transfer below. You may use some words more than once.

electrically   mechanically   heating   by light or sound

a   Boiling a pan of water on a gas stove transfers energy from a chemical store
to a thermal store. _____

b   A catapult transfers energy from its elastic store to the kinetic store of the ball.

_____

c   Rolling a ball down a slope transfers energy from the gravitational potential store
to the thermal store of the surroundings. _____

d   A light bulb transfers energy from the chemical store in coal at the power station
to the thermal store of the surroundings

15.2 Energy conservation

1 What is the law of conservation of energy?

The law tells us that energy cannot be _____

2 Complete the table to show if each energy transfer is useful or wasted.

	Energy transfer	Useful or wasted?
a	When a car is being driven, some energy is transferred as sound to the surroundings	
b	When a hairdryer is being used, energy is transferred to the thermal store of the heating element in the hairdryer	
c	When a drill is being used, energy is transferred to the kinetic store of the drill	
d	When you rub cold hands together, friction between your hands causes energy to be transferred to the thermal store of your hands	

3 When you brake, friction acts between the wheel and the brake pad.

What would you expect to happen to the thermal store (the temperature) of the brake pad

during braking? _____

4 How can you reduce friction in machinery? _____

15.3 Energy transfer by heating

1 Students did an experiment to measure the thermal conductivity of some materials as shown in the diagram.

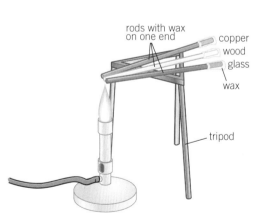

a Which rod would you expect the wax to melt on?

_____

b Would that rod have the highest or lowest thermal conductivity?

_____

2 Students tested four different types of insulation in the gap between two beakers, as shown in the diagram.

The temperature of the water at the start of the experiment was 90 °C.

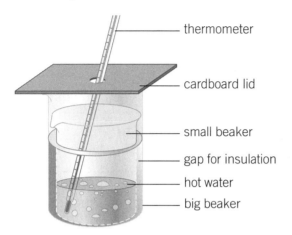

Material	Temperature of the water at the end of the investigation (°C)
Air	62
Cotton wool	72
Felt	74
Sawdust	68

a   Which material was the best insulator? _____

b   Which material was the worst insulator? _____

3 Modern homes are built with two layers of brick with a gap (a cavity) between them.

How can you reduce the heat lost through a wall cavity?

_____

15.4 Energy resources

1 Some of our energy resources will eventually run out and some will never run out.

Draw **one** line from each type of energy resource to whether it will run out or not.

Type of energy resource

Renewable

Non-renewable

Will it run out?

Will never run out

Will eventually run out

2 Complete the table to show if the energy resources are renewable or non-renewable.

Draw **one** tick in each row.

	Energy resource	Renewable	Non-renewable
a	fossil fuels		
b	solar power		
c	nuclear power		
d	wind power		
e	hydroelectric power (from running water)		

3 Put the stages of making electricity in a power station into the correct order.

	What happens
A	Water turns from a liquid to steam (gas).
B	The turbine turns the generator.
C	Fossil fuel is burned (OR nuclear fuel undergoes nuclear fission) to heat the water.
D	Steam turns the turbine.
E	Electricity is generated.

Correct order: ☐ ☐ ☐ ☐ ☐

Now I know:	☹	😐	☺
The ways energy can be stored and how energy can be transferred between stores			
How to identify useful energy transfers			
What is meant by wasted energy and how to reduce it			
What is meant by thermal conductivity and how to recognise the materials with the highest and lowest thermal conductivity			
What is meant by renewable and non-renewable energy resources			

Key words

efficiency   carbon capture   global warming   acid rain

15.5 Energy efficiency

1 The efficiency of an appliance tells us how much of the input energy is transferred usefully.

What unit is used for input energy? Tick **one** box.

Joules (J) ☐   Percent (%) ☐   Seconds (s) ☐   Watts (W) ☐

2 We calculate the efficiency of an appliance as a percentage.

Which of the following is the correct equation for calculating efficiency? _____

A $\text{efficiency} = \dfrac{\text{useful output energy}}{\text{total input energy}}$

B $\text{efficiency} = \dfrac{\text{useful output energy}}{\text{total input energy}} \times 100$

C $\text{efficiency} = \dfrac{\text{total input energy}}{\text{total output energy}} \times 100$

D $\text{efficiency} = \dfrac{\text{total input energy}}{\text{total output energy}}$

3 The efficiency of four types of light bulb are shown below.

Tick the bulb that transfers the lowest amount of input energy to wasted output energy.

Filament bulb – 10%   ☐

Energy-saving fluorescent bulb – 85%   ☐

LED lighting – 90%   ☐

Fluorescent strip lighting – 50%   ☐

4 Why are we being encouraged to switch to bulbs that are more efficient?

_____

15.6 Energy and the environment

1 a Which greenhouse gas is produced when we burn fossil fuels?

_____

b How would carbon capture affect the amount of this gas being released?

_____

2 Burning some fossil fuels also produces sulfur dioxide and oxides of nitrogen.

What is the type of pollution created when these gases dissolve in rainwater?

_____

3 a Give **one** advantage of nuclear power.

It doesn't produce _____

b Give **one** disadvantage of nuclear power.

The waste it produces is _____

4 Here are five facts about renewable energy resources. Tick the facts that are advantages.

A	Some sources, like solar cells and wind turbines, need large areas of land to generate lots of power	
B	They never run out	
C	They can be unreliable – it isn't always windy or sunny when we need to generate electricity	
D	They don't produce greenhouse gases	
E	Building turbines and hydroelectric dams can affect the habitat of local animals and plants	

Now I know:	☹	😐	☺
How to recognise the input energy and output energy of a device			
What is meant by efficiency and how to work it out			
The problems associated with fossil fuels and nuclear power (non-renewable sources)			
The advantages and disadvantages of renewable energy resources			

16 Forces and work

Key words

force	newtons	contact	non-contact	work	friction

16.1 Forces

1 Use the correct answers from the box to complete the sentence about what a force is.

force	object	object	pull	push	work

A force is a _____ or a _____

that acts on an _____ because of another _____ .

2 These arrows represent forces.

A	B	C	D	E
→	↓	↓	↑	↑

a Which two arrows could represent gravitational force?

_____ and _____

b Which arrow shows the largest gravitational force? _____

3 Put each of the forces below into the correct categories.

air resistance	friction	gravitational force	magnetic	tension

Contact force	Non-contact force

4 Tick the correct unit we use to measure forces.

Centimetres (cm) ☐   Joules (J) ☐   Newtons (N) ☐   Watts (W) ☐

16.2 Work done

1 When a force makes an object move, we say that work is done.

What is the unit for work done? _____

2 When you push a box across the floor, a force acts in the opposite direction, as shown on the diagram.

What is the name of this force that acts in the opposite direction to movement?

_____

3 When you rub your hands together, the force you named in question **2** causes a change in temperature as you do work to overcome it.

What happens to the temperature of your hands?

_____

4 This diagram shows a car on a road.

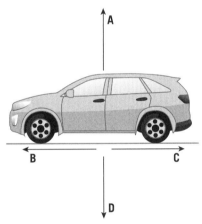

Which of the labelled arrows represents the force named in question **2**? _____

Now I know:	☹	😐	☺
What is meant by a force			
The unit used to measure forces			
What is meant by work (in science)			
What friction is			

Key words

weight   gravitational field strength   power   watts   elastic
inelastic   limit of proportionality   directly proportional

16.3 Weight

1 Your weight is due to the gravitational force of the Earth pulling you down. Your mass is due to the number of atoms in your body.

Which would change in space, your weight or your mass? _____

2 a What is the unit used to measure weight? _____

   b What is the unit used to measure mass? _____

3 If you know the gravitational field strength you can calculate the weight.

Which of these is the correct formula to calculate weight? _____

A $\text{weight} = \dfrac{\text{mass}}{\text{gravitational field strength}}$

B weight = mass × gravitational field strength

C $\text{weight} = \dfrac{\text{gravitational field strength}}{\text{mass}}$

D weight = mass × force

4 The gravitational field strength of the Earth is 10 N/kg and the gravitational field strength of Mercury is 3.8 N/kg

On which of these planets would you weigh more? _____

16.4 Work done and power

1 When a force is applied to an object and it moves, work is done.
Which of these is the correct formula for calculating the work done? _____

A work done $= \dfrac{\text{force}}{\text{distance moved}}$

B work = force × gravitational field strength

C work done $= \dfrac{\text{distance moved}}{\text{force}}$

D work = force × distance moved

2 Power is how much work you do in an amount of time.
Tick the unit that power is measured in.

Centimetres (cm) ☐   Joules (J) ☐   Newtons (N) ☐   Watt (W) ☐

3 Two runners ran the same distance of 200 m.
Runner A took 3 minutes and runner B took 5 minutes.

Which runner had the most power? _____

4 Which of these is the correct formula for power? _____

A power $= \dfrac{\text{time}}{\text{work done}}$

B power = work done × time

C power $= \dfrac{\text{work done}}{\text{time}}$

D power = force × time

16.5 Forces and elasticity

1 Draw **one** line from each term to the correct definition.

Term	Definition
Elastic	Doesn't return to its original shape or size after stretching
Inelastic	Returns to original shape or size after stretching

2 Students investigated how different materials stretched using the equipment shown. They collected the results shown in the graph.

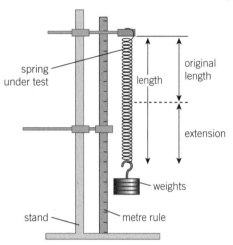

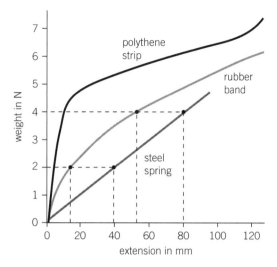

a Write down the equation to calculate the extension of a material.

b For which material was the force applied *directly proportional* to the extension?

Circle the correct material.

polythene strip   rubber band   steel spring

c Which of the materials showed the greatest extension when a force of 4 N was applied?

_____

d When the students added even more weights (increasing the force), the spring was stretched beyond its limit of proportionality.

What happened to the spring when they removed these weights?

_____

Now I know:	☹	😐	☺
What weight is and how to calculate it			
The difference between weight and mass (the definition for each)			
How to calculate the work done			
What power is, the units of power, and how to calculate it			
What is meant by being elastic or inelastic			

17 Speed and stopping distances

Key words

speed   braking distance   thinking distance   stopping distance

17.1 Speed

1 Speed is a measurement of how fast something is moving.

Tick the correct unit for speed.

s/m ☐   m/s ☐   m/s² ☐   J/s ☐

2 What is the formula you use to calculate the speed of a moving object? _____

A speed = $\dfrac{\text{distance}}{\text{time}}$ B speed = $\dfrac{\text{time}}{\text{distance}}$

C speed = distance × time   D speed = time × distance²

3 Average speed cameras see a car at two points on a road and then calculate the average speed of that car.

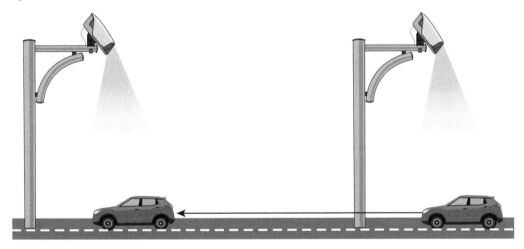

Tick the **one** statement that is true to avoid a speeding ticket on this road.

A Drivers must drive consistently below the speed limit. ☐

B Drivers can drive a little over the limit for a very short time if they then stick to the speed limit. ☐

C Drivers can drive a little over the limit for a very short time if they then drive below the speed limit. ☐

17.2 Braking distance

1 The time taken for a car to stop is made up of the thinking distance and the braking distance.

What happens to the stopping distance if the speed increases?

_____

2 Does drinking alcohol increase or decrease someone's thinking distance?

_____

3 The braking distance is the time it takes to stop the car once the brakes have been applied.

What effect would lowering the friction between the road and wheels (e.g. ice on road) have on the braking distance?

The braking distance would _____

4 Apart from friction, name **one** other factor that could affect the braking distance of the car.

_____

Now I know:	☹	😐	☺
What speed is and how to calculate it			
That stopping distance is made of the thinking distance and the braking distance			
The factors that affect the stopping distance and the thinking distance			

17.3 Distance–time graphs

1   Look at the distance–time graph of a baby crawling along the floor.

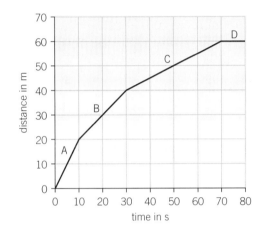

a   Which letter on the graph shows when it has stopped moving? _____

b   Which letter on the graph shows when it is moving fastest? _____

c   Which letter on the graph shows when it is moving slowest? _____

d   Which letter on the graph shows when it travels 20 m in 20 s? _____

e   Calculate the speed of the baby from part **d**. Include the units.

_____ Units: _____

f   Calculate the average speed of the baby (over 80 s). Include the units.

_____ Units: _____

2   Is distance a vector quantity (direction and size) or a scalar quantity (size)? _____

17.4 Investigating acceleration

1 Acceleration has both a quantity and a direction.

Is acceleration a vector or a scalar quantity? _____

2 Tick the correct unit for acceleration.

m ☐   m/s ☐   m/s² ☐   J/s ☐

3 What is the correct formula for acceleration? _____

A $acceleration = \dfrac{distance}{time}$ B $acceleration = \dfrac{change\ in\ velocity}{time}$

C acceleration = change in velocity × time   D acceleration = time × distance²

4 You can use the equipment shown in the diagram to measure acceleration.

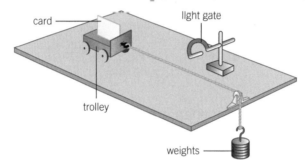

Put the stages of the investigation into the correct order.

	Instructions
A	Mark the start point.
B	Calculate the acceleration, using the final velocity (minus the starting velocity of zero), and the time taken to reach the light gate.
C	Release the trolley and time how long it takes to reach the light gate (this is the time taken for the velocity to change).
D	Set up apparatus. Put 0.2 N on the hanger.
E	Record the velocity measured by the light gate and data logger. You will have to put in the length of the card so the data logger can calculate the final velocity of the trolley.

Correct order: ☐ ☐ ☐ ☐ ☐

17.5 Speed–time graphs

1 The graph shows a runner setting off on their morning run.

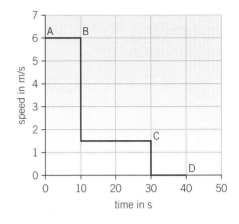

Between which points on the graph does the runner:

a walk at constant speed? _____

b run at constant speed? _____

c stop for a rest? _____

2 Below is a speed–time graph for a car.

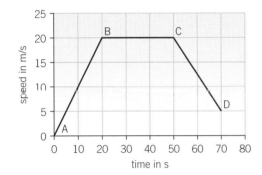

a Between which two points is there no acceleration? _____

b Between which two points is the car decelerating? _____

c Between which two points is the car accelerating? _____

d Calculate the acceleration between the points in part **c**.

_____ m/s²

Now I know:	🙁	😐	🙂
How to read a distance–time graph, recognising when something is moving or stationary			
Acceleration is a change in velocity, and the formula to calculate it			
How to measure acceleration in an investigation			
How to recognise acceleration, deceleration, and movement at a constant speed on a speed–time graph			

18 Atoms and nuclear radiation

Key words

ionising radiation   unstable   alpha   beta   gamma   Geiger counter   detect

18.1 Atoms and radiation

1   Label this diagram of an atom using the correct answers from the box.

> electron   neutron   nucleus   proton

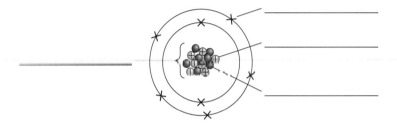

2   List the three types of ionising radiation.

1 _____   2 _____   3 _____

3   What is the name given to the process when an atom breaks down
    and emits ionising radiation?

R _____   d _____

4   Tick **two** boxes that show ways to detect ionising radiation.

With a radio detector   ☐   With photographic film   ☐

With a mobile phone camera   ☐   With a Geiger counter   ☐

18.2 Alpha, beta, and gamma radiation

1   Write whether the following types of ionising radiation are alpha, beta, or gamma.

a   An electromagnetic wave. _____

b   A large particle of protons and neutrons. _____

c   A small particle – an electron. _____

2 Draw **one** line from each type of ionising radiation to how far it can travel in air and to the material that absorbs it.

Type of ionising radiation	Range in air	Material needed to absorb it
Alpha	About 1 m	A 5 mm thick piece of aluminium
Beta	Unlimited	A thin sheet of paper
Gamma	About 5 cm	A thick sheet of lead or about a metre of concrete

3 Ionising radiation is dangerous because it can knock electrons out of an atom.

What can happen if these electrons are knocked out of a DNA molecule?

Damage to the DNA molecule can cause _____

4 Which type of radiation is the most ionising (the most damaging)? _____

5 People who work with radiation need to take safety precautions.

Name **two** safety precautions that a radiation worker could take.

1 _____ 2 _____

18.3 Using radiation

1 Alpha radiation can be used in smoke alarms (like the one shown).

Put these steps in the right order to explain how a smoke alarm works.

	What happens
A	Smoke enters the smoke alarm and absorbs the radiation.
B	Alpha particles ionise the radiation in the smoke alarm helping to make an electric circuit.
C	The smoke alarm goes off.
D	The electric circuit is broken.

Correct order: ☐ ☐ ☐ ☐

2 Why aren't we in any danger from the alpha radiation inside a smoke alarm?

_____

3 Beta radiation can be used to monitor the thickness of metal foil when it is being made.

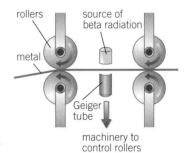

a If the sheet of foil is too thick, what will happen to the amount of beta radiation detected by the Geiger tube?

_____

b What happens to the amount of beta radiation detected if the foil is too thin?

_____

4 Gamma radiation can be used as a medical tracer.

A doctor injects a source of gamma radiation into a patient.

This radioactive source is followed around the body by measuring the gamma radiation.

a Why is gamma radiation safer to use inside the body than alpha or beta radiation?

_____

b If alpha radiation was used inside the body it wouldn't be detected outside the body. Why wouldn't it be detected?

_____

Now I know:	☹	😐	☺
What is meant by the term 'ionising radiation'			
The names of the three different types of ionising radiation			
The materials required to absorb the three types of ionising radiation			
Uses of the three types of ionising radiation			

18.4 Half-life

1   The activity of a radioactive source is a measure of how many
    unstable nuclei decay (break up) each second.

    Tick the correct unit for activity.

    becquerels (Bq) ☐   hertz (Hz) ☐   joules (J) ☐   watts (W) ☐

2   We can measure activity of a source over time by measuring the half-life.

    What is the half-life of a radioactive source?

    The half-life is the time taken for _____

3   The graph shows the decay of a radioactive source.

    What is the half-life for this source? Circle the correct letter.

    W   0 minutes

    X   2 minutes

    Y   4 minutes

    Z   6 minutes

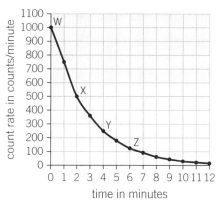

4   Some elements exist in different forms called isotopes (e.g. carbon-12 and carbon-14).
    Different radioactive isotopes can have different half-lives.

    Tick what differs between isotopes of the same element.

    Number of protons ☐   Number of electrons ☐

    Number of neutrons ☐   Number of electron shells ☐

18.5 Radioactive contamination

1 Draw **one** line between each term and its description.

Term	Definition
Radioactive contamination	The time it takes for the activity of a radioactive source to fall to half of its initial value
Half-life	The presence of radioactive materials where they shouldn't be
Irradiation	The exposure of an object to ionising radiation

2 Food that has been sterilised by irradiation with gamma rays has this symbol on the packaging.

a Are things that have been irradiated in this way radioactive?

_____

b Is it safe to eat food that has been irradiated? _____

c Give an example of something else that might be sterilised by exposure to gamma rays. _____

3 Contamination is a risk to those people who work with radioactive substances.

The level of risk depends on the half-life of the source and the type of radiation emitted.

How will the half-life of the radioactive substance affect the risk?

Radioactive substances with a long half-life will be _____

_____

Now I know:	☹	😐	☺
What is meant by the term half-life			
What the difference is between different isotopes of the same element			
What is meant by radioactive contamination			
What is meant by the term irradiation and examples of irradiation in industry			

1. The diagram shows a way of generating electricity.

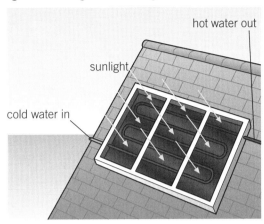

a   What type of energy resource is this?   **[1 mark]**

Draw a ring around **one** answer.

coal   **nuclear**   **solar**

b   Is this a renewable or non-renewable way of generating electricity?   **[1 mark]**

....

2. A hairdryer transfers energy.

Some of the energy transfers are useful.

Energy not transferred to a useful energy store is wasted.

Which of these is a wasted energy transfer?   **[1 mark]**

Tick (✓) **one** box.

Increase in kinetic store of fan   ☐

Increase in thermal store of heater   ☐

Increase in the thermal store of your hair   ☐

Sound energy transferred to the surroundings   ☐

3. a   Tick **one** box for each statement about forces to say if it is true or false.   **[4 marks]**

Statement	True	False
Force is measured in newtons (N).		
Friction is a force that can cause objects to cool down.		
Friction is a non-contact force.		
When a force makes an object move, we say that work is done on the object.		

b Which of these is **not** a force? [1 mark]

Tick (✓) **one** box.

Electricity ☐

Friction ☐

Magnetism ☐

4. An athlete throws a ball into the air.

a At which point on the diagram is the gravitational potential energy at its greatest?

Tick (✓) **one** box. [1 mark]

X ☐

Y ☐

Z ☐

b Use the correct answers from the box to complete the sentences below. [2 marks]

elastic	gravitational potential

When the athlete releases the ball, its .... energy is greatest.

kinetic	thermal

Then as the ball gets higher in the air, the .... store of the ball increases.

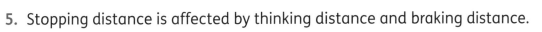

5. Stopping distance is affected by thinking distance and braking distance.

   a   Draw one line from the distance to the correct definition.   [1 mark]

   Distance

   | Thinking distance |

   | Braking distance |

   Definition

   | Distance a car travels once the breaks have been applied |

   | Distance a car travels whilst the driver reacts |

   b   What is one factor that affects **both** thinking and braking distance?   [1 mark]

   Circle **one** answer.

   alcohol   **condition of tyres**   **speed of car**

   c   In which weather conditions would the braking distance be highest?   [1 mark]

   Tick (✓) **one** box.

   Fog   ☐

   Rain   ☐

   Sun   ☐

   d   What is the name of the force that stops a car when it applies the breaks?   [1 mark]

   ....

6. The diagram shows a cheetah running.

   a   The cheetah runs 125 metres in 5 seconds.

       Calculate the speed of the cheetah.   [2 marks]

       Use the equation speed = $\frac{\text{distance}}{\text{time}}$

       ....

   b   What is the correct unit for the speed of the cheetah?   [1 mark]

       Draw a circle around the correct answer.

       ms   **m/s**   **s/m**

c The cheetah starts to slow down.

Draw two arrows to show the forces working on the cheetah as it slows down. **[2 marks]**

7. Some atomic nuclei emit radiation.

There are three types of nuclear radiation: alpha, beta, and gamma.

Each type of radiation has different penetrating power.

a Mark on the diagram where you would be able to detect beta radiation, but not alpha radiation.

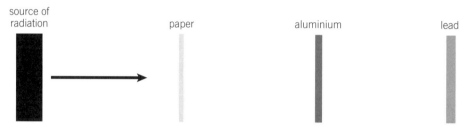

b What is one use of gamma radiation? **[1 mark]**

Tick (✓) **one** box.

Medical tracer ☐

Monitor thickness of metal foil ☐

Smoke detector ☐

c What is one danger of using gamma radiation? **[1 mark]**

....

8. A student investigated the effectiveness of three types of insulation.

They heated some water in a beaker to 50 °C. They wrapped the beaker in cotton wool then measured how long it took for the temperature to drop to 25 °C.

They repeated the experiment using cardboard, and with no insulation.

a The diagram shows the experimental set up.

Label, on the diagram, the piece of apparatus used to measure temperature. **[1 mark]**

b The graph shows the student's results.

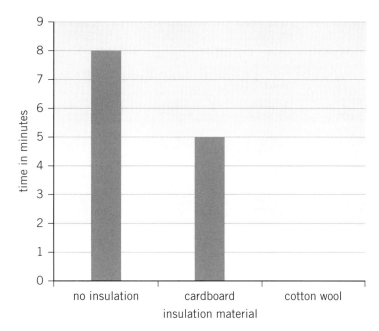

How long did it take the beaker wrapped in cardboard to cool? **[1 mark]**

....

c It took 4 minutes for the beaker wrapped in cotton wool to cool.

Complete the bar chart by drawing the bar for cotton wool. **[1 mark]**

d Which insulation material was the most effective? **[1 mark]**

....

Component 5: Exam-style questions (Trilogy)

01 We need a range of energy resources to generate electricity for a growing population.

01.1 Is nuclear fuel an example of a renewable or non-renewable energy source? **[1 mark]**

Circle the correct answer.

Renewable **Non-renewable**

01.2 Nuclear fuel does not produce greenhouse gases such as carbon dioxide.

What is one disadvantage of using nuclear fuel? **[1 mark]**

____

02 **Figure 1** shows an atom of carbon-12.

Figure 1

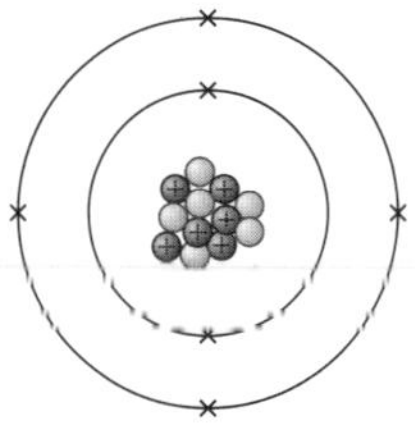

02.1 What is the mass number of this carbon atom? **[1 mark]**

Tick **one** box.

6 ☐

10 ☐

12 ☐

14 ☐

02.2 What is the atomic number of this carbon atom? **[1 mark]**

Tick **one** box.

6 ☐

10 ☐

12 ☐

14 ☐

02.3 Carbon-14 is another isotope of carbon.

Describe how an atom of carbon-14 is different from an atom of carbon-12. **[1 mark]**

____

02.4 Carbon-14 is radioactive.

We can use the amount of carbon-14 in a specimen to work out when it died.

Figure 2 shows the radioactive decay curve for carbon-14.

Figure 2

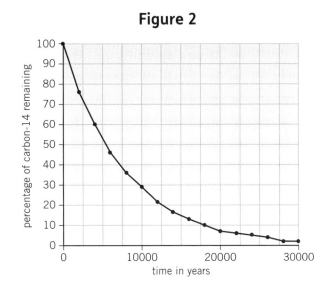

What is the half-life of carbon-14? [1 mark]

_____

03 The activity of a source is the number of unstable nuclei that decay each second.

What is the unit we use to measure radioactive activity? [1 mark]

_____

04 Weight is the force acting on an object due to gravity.

04.1 What is the unit of weight? [1 mark]

Tick **one** box.

Joules (J) ☐

Kilograms (kg) ☐

Newtons (N) ☐

Watts (W) ☐

04.2 **Table 1** shows the gravitational field strength of different planets.

Table 1

Planet	Gravitational field strength in N/kg
Mercury	3.8
Venus	8.8
Jupiter	25.0
Saturn	10.4

On which planet would an astronaut have the greatest weight? **[1 mark]**

_____

04.3 Calculate the weight of an object on Mercury. The mass of the object is 50 kg.

Use the equation weight = mass × gravitational field strength. **[2 marks]**

_____

05 When a force is applied to an object and it moves, work is done.

05.1 Write the equation that links work done, force, and distance. **[1 mark]**

05.2 Calculate the work done when 50 N of force is applied to an object over 15 metres. **[2 marks]**

_____

06 A dog walker is walking in the countryside.

She follows a winding path and changes speed during the walk.

Figure 3 shows the distance the dog walker covered on the walk.

Figure 3

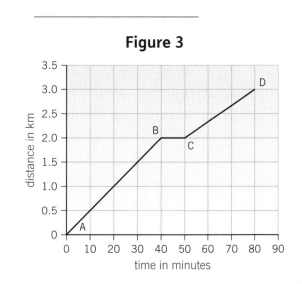

06.1 Speed is a scalar quantity.

What is the equation for speed that links distance and time? **[1 mark]**

06.2 Between which two points on the graph did the dog walker stop to play fetch with the dog?

Tick **one** box. **[1 mark]**

A–B ☐

B–C ☐

C–D ☐

06.3 How far did the dog walker walk? **[1 mark]**

_____ km

06.4 **Figure 4** shows the speed of the dog walker plotted against time for a typical walk.

Figure 4

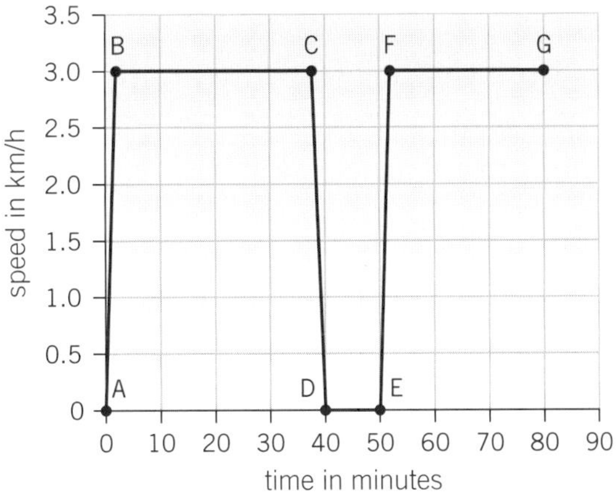

Between which two points was the dog walker stationary (standing still)?

Tick **one** box. **[1 mark]**

A–B ☐

B–C ☐

C–D ☐

D–E ☐

06.5 Define the term 'acceleration'. **[1 mark]**

_____

06.6 Between which points was the walker accelerating?

Tick **one** box. [1 mark]

A–B ☐

B–C ☐

C–D ☐

D–E ☐

07 A ball is rolling down a hill. The ball is accelerating.

07.1 Draw arrows on **Figure 5** to show the forces acting on the ball. [2 marks]

Figure 5

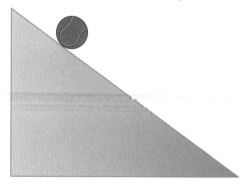

07.2 Choose the correct words from the box to complete the sentence. [2 marks]

| elastic | gravitational potentital | kinetic | thermal |

As the ball rolls down the hill, energy is transferred from _____
energy store to _____ energy store.

08 A student investigated the extension of a spring.

Their results are shown in **Table 2**.

Table 2

Weight in N	Original length in mm	New length in mm	Extension in mm
1	50	60	10
2	50	85	35
3	50	105	
4	50	130	80
5	50	160	110

08.1 Calculate the missing extension and fill in **Table 2**.   [1 mark]

08.2 The student plotted their results on a graph (**Figure 6**).

Plot the missing extension onto the graph.   [1 mark]

Figure 6

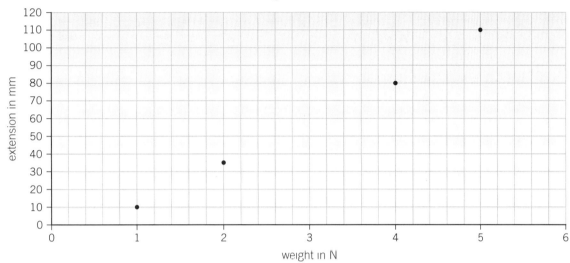

weight in N

09 A toaster uses 800 joules of energy per second.

600 joules of the energy is used to toast the bread. This is the useful output energy.

09.1 Calculate the efficiency of the toaster.   [2 marks]

Use the equation efficiency $= \dfrac{\text{useful output energy}}{\text{total input energy}} \times 100$

_____

09.2 Student A says the rest of the energy is not transferred as useful output energy.

Student B says the rest of the energy is destroyed.

Which student is correct? Give a reason for your answer.   [2 marks]

_____

_____

19 Electrical current

Key words

current   voltage   amps   volts   charge   ammeter
voltmeter   direct current   alternating current

19.1 Electrical current

1   We often need to measure the flow of electric charge in a circuit.

What is the name of this flow? _____

2   a   Draw **one** line from each meter to the units it measures.

Device	The unit
Ammeter	Volts
Voltmeter	Amps

b   What does an ammeter measure? _____

c   What does a voltmeter measure? _____

3   The circuit shows a bulb and an ammeter connected to a cell.
The wire has been cut as shown.

a   How does the cut wire affect the bulb?

_____

b   How does the cut wire affect the reading on the ammeter?

_____

4   Scientists often want to know the resistance of an electrical component.

Complete the following sentence.

The resistance is how _____ it is for the current to pass through a component.

Increasing the resistance in a circuit will _____ the current passing through it.

19.2 Types of current

1 Electrical current is the flow of charge.

What is the unit we use to measure electric charge? _____

2 Draw **one** line from each type of electric current to its description.

Type of current   **Description**

| Direct current (dc) | | The charge keeps moving in the same direction |

| Alternating current (ac) | | The charge constantly changes direction |

3 The diagrams show two oscilloscope screens.

A 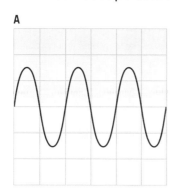   B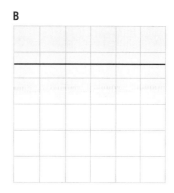

  a   Which screen shows ac? _____

  b   Which screen shows dc? _____

4 a   Is mains electricity in our homes alternating current or direct current? _____

  b   What is the voltage of mains electricity? _____

  c   Does a cell in a circuit produce ac or dc current?
      Circle the correct answer.

      ac   dc

Now I know:	☹	😐	☺
What voltage and current measure, and the units for each			
How increasing the resistance affects the flow of current			
The difference between alternating and direct current			
An example of where you would use alternating and direct current			

resistance   ohms   series circuits   parallel circuits

thermistor   diode   light-dependent resistor (LDR)

19.3 Resistance

1   Resistance is the measure of how difficult it is for a current to flow through a component.

Tick the correct unit for resistance.

Amps (A) ☐   Hertz (Hz) ☐   Ohms (Ω) ☐   Volts (V) ☐

2   Which is the correct formula for calculating the resistance? _____

A   resistance = $\dfrac{\text{potential difference}}{\text{current}}$ C   resistance = current × potential difference

B   resistance = $\dfrac{\text{current}}{\text{potential difference}}$ D   resistance = current – potential difference

3   The resistance of the wire is affected by temperature.

Will increasing the temperature increase or decrease the resistance? _____

19.4 Investigating components

1   We can measure the current–voltage characteristics of different components using the circuit shown.

Put the stages of the investigation in the correct order.

A	Record voltage and current.
B	Connect up the circuit and place the component to be tested in place.
C	Repeat for several different settings on the variable resistor.
D	Move the dial on the variable resistor to a new position and measure voltage and current.
E	Repeat for a different component.

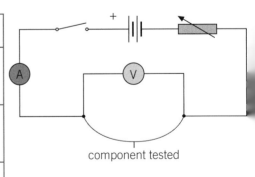
component tested

Correct order: ☐☐☐☐☐

2 Draw **one** line from each component to its description.

Component	Description
Filament lamp	Lights up and gets hotter as it is used.
Resistor	Only allows the current to flow in one direction.
Diode	Resistance decreases as light intensity or temperature increases.
Thermistor and Light-dependent resistors (LDR)	Resists the flow of electric current (depending on the resistance).

3 The graphs show current–voltage characteristics for some common circuit components.

Write the name of the component under the correct graph.

diode   filament lamp   resistor

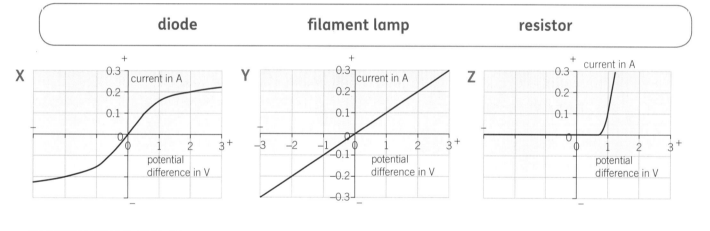

_____   _____   _____

19.5 Series and parallel circuits

1 Draw **one** line to match each circuit type to its example.

Type of circuit

Example

| Series circuit |

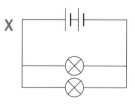

X

| Parallel circuit |

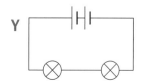

Y

2 Which circuit in question **1** would have the brightest bulbs? _____

3 The diagram shows a bulb connected to a battery.

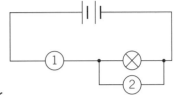

   a Which number shows where you would put an ammeter in the circuit? _____

   b Which number shows where you would put a voltmeter in the circuit? _____

4 Complete the table to show whether each statement is true or false. Tick **one** box in each row.

	Statement	True	False
A	In a series circuit, different amounts of current will flow through each bulb.		
B	In a series circuit, the voltage is shared between the two bulbs.		
C	In a parallel circuit, the total current can be calculated by adding up the current flowing through each bulb.		
D	In a parallel circuit, the voltage for each bulb is the same voltage as the power supply.		
E	The resistance of a parallel circuit increases as you add more components.		
F	Adding more components to a series circuit will decrease the resistance.		

Now I know:	☹	😐	☺
The equation to calculate resistance and the units of resistance			
How to measure resistance in a piece of wire			
How to measure the current–voltage characteristics of some different components			
The current–voltage characteristic graphs of a lamp, a resistor, and a diode			
How to recognise series and parallel circuits			
How voltage, current, and resistance are different in a series and a parallel circuit			

20 Domestic electricity

Key words

earth   neutral   live   fuse   power

20.1 Wiring a plug

1   The wires in a plug are each a different colour.

Draw **one** line to match each wire to its colour.

Name of wire	Colour
Earth wire	Brown
Neutral wire	Blue
Live wire	Green and yellow stripes

2   The diagram shows a UK three-pin plug.

Complete the table with the labels below to name each part of the plug.

cable grip   earth wire   fuse   live wire   neutral wire

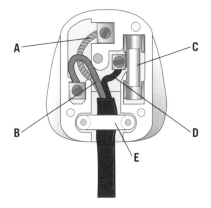

Label	Part of plug
A	
B	
C	
D	
E	

3   How does a fuse keep us safe?

If too much current passes through the fuse it will _____

_____

20.2 Fuses and earth wires

1 Appliances with a metal case have an earth wire as shown in the diagram.

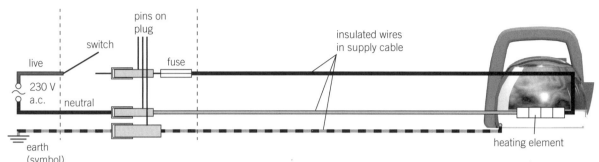

Complete the flowchart to show how an earth wire keeps you safe.

a The earth wire is connected to the _____ and the _____ .

↓

b If there is a fault, the electric current will flow _____.

↓

c When electricity flows to earth, the fuse should _____ and the current will

_____.

↓

d If there was a fault and no earth wire, the electric current would flow

_____, causing _____.

2 Sometimes an appliance has this symbol
which tells us the appliance is double insulated.
How does double insulation keep us safe?

_____

3 Most household plugs contain a fuse. Tick the fuse values below that are used in the UK.

1 A ☐   3 A ☐   5 A ☐

10 A ☐   13 A ☐   15 A ☐

4 It is important to use the correct type of fuse in an appliance.

a What would happen if you use a fuse with a rating too low for the appliance you are
using? _____

b What would happen if you use a fuse with a rating too high for the appliance it is
protecting? _____

20.3 Transferring energy

1 We use the term power to describe how fast an appliance is at transferring energy.

Tick the correct unit for power.

amps (A) ☐   joules (J) ☐   volts (V) ☐   watts (W) ☐

2 Which is the correct equation for calculating energy transferred by an appliance? _____

A energy transferred = $\dfrac{voltage}{current}$ B energy transferred = $\dfrac{power}{time}$

C energy transferred = $\dfrac{time}{power}$ D Energy transferred = power × time

3 The table shows the power of several appliances.

Appliance	Power rating in W
Refrigerator	200
Tumble drier	2500

Appliance	Power rating in W
Mobile phone charger	10
Fan heater	1000

Tick the statements below that are true.

A   The tumble drier will cost the most to run   ☐

B   The mobile phone charger is the least powerful   ☐

C   The tumble drier will require the largest fuse   ☐

D   The fan heater will require the smallest fuse   ☐

E   The fan heater is the most powerful   ☐

4 We pay the electricity companies for the energy transferred in our homes.

What is the unit used to calculate our electricity bills? _____

Now I know:	☹	😐	☺
The names and colours of the three wires used to connect electrical appliances			
How to wire a three pin plug			
How fuses and the earth wire keep us safe			
The units used by electricity companies to measure energy transfers in our home			

National Grid   transformers

20.4 Power

1 Complete this sentence.

The power of an appliance is the amount of energy _____.

2 Which of these is the correct equation for calculating power? _____

A $\text{power} = \dfrac{\text{energy transferred}}{\text{time}}$

B $\text{power} = \dfrac{\text{current}}{\text{time}}$

C $\text{power} = \dfrac{\text{time}}{\text{energy transferred}}$

D $\text{power} = \text{energy transferred} \times \text{time}$

3 Which of these can be used to calculate power of an electrical appliance? _____

A $\text{power} = \dfrac{\text{potential difference}}{\text{current}}$

B $\text{power} = \dfrac{\text{current}}{\text{time}}$

C $\text{power} = \text{potential difference} \times \text{time}$

D $\text{power} = \text{potential difference} \times \text{current}$

20.5 The National Grid

1 The National Grid is a system of cables and transformers linking power stations to places that use electricity.

Draw **one** line from each part of the Grid to its function.

Part of the National Grid	Function
Power station	These allow electrical current to flow to where it is needed
Step-up transformer	These decrease the potential difference
Step-down transformer	These generate electricity
Transmission cables	These increase the potential difference

2 The diagram shows the stages in the National Grid.

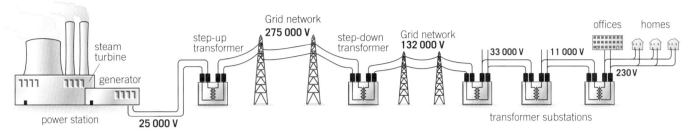

Put the steps for how the National Grid works into the correct order.

A The potential difference is decreased using a series of step-down transformers.

B Electrical current flows along the transmission cables. Many of these are suspended from pylons.

C Electricity is generated at the power station at 25 000 V.

D Electricity is ready to be used in homes and offices (usually at 230 V).

E The potential difference is increased using a step-up transformer to 275 000 V.

Correct order: [C] [ ] [ ] [ ] [ ]

3 Why do we use very high potential differences in the National Grid even though they are dangerous to life?

Circle the correct words to complete the sentences.

Using a high potential difference means that a **smaller / larger** current will flow,

which **reduces / increases** energy transfer to the thermal store of the cable and the surroundings.

This **decreases / increases** the efficiency of the National Grid.

Now I know:	☹	😐	☺
The equations we can use to calculate the power of an appliance			
The main parts of the National Grid			
Why we use large potential differences in the National Grid			

181

21 Magnetism and electromagnetism

Key words

permanent magnet   electromagnet   magnetic field   attract   repel   solenoid   relay

21.1 Magnetic fields

1   Circle the kind of force exerted by a magnet: **contact**   **non-contact**

2   The diagram shows four pairs of magnets.

   For each pair, say if the magnets would attract or repel.

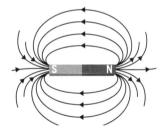

W _____

X _____

Y _____

Z _____

3   We can use iron filings to show the magnetic field lines around a magnet.

   Draw **one** line from each diagram to its description.

Diagram	Description
X 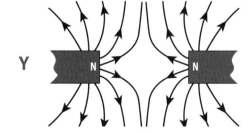	The magnetic field when two like poles meet.
Y	The magnetic field around a bar magnet.
Z 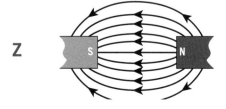	The magnetic field when two opposite poles meet.

21.2 Magnetic fields around an electric current

1 When a current flows through a wire, a magnetic field is produced around it.

How would the following changes affect the strength of the magnetic field?

a Increasing the current: _____

b Increasing the distance from the wire: _____

2 The diagrams show magnetic field patterns.

Draw **one** line from each diagram to its description.

Diagram   **Description**

X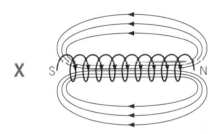

The magnetic field pattern around a wire.

Y

The magnetic field pattern around a solenoid.

3 A solenoid is a long coil of insulated wire.

What do you call a solenoid with an iron core? _____

21.3 Electromagnets

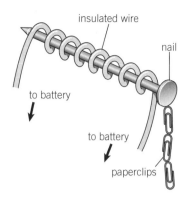

1 You can make a simple electromagnet by wrapping insulated wire around a nail as shown in the diagram.

    a How would increasing the number of coils of wire affect the number of paperclips picked up? _____

    b What other factor would affect the number of paperclips picked up? _____

2 A crane in a scrapyard might use an electromagnet to move large pieces of magnetic metal. What is the advantage of using an electromagnet instead of a permanent magnet to pick up cars?

_____

3 The diagram shows a type of switch called a relay.

Put the statements in order to show how the relay works.

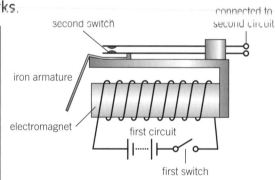

A	The iron armature is attracted by the magnetic field.
B	An electric current flows through the second circuit.
C	This completes the second circuit.
D	The first switch is turned on and electric current flows around the coil.

Correct order: ☐ ☐ ☐ ☐

Now I know:	☹	😐	☺
Which combination of magnetic poles will attract and repel			
What the magnetic field looks like around a bar magnet			
How we can change the strength of the magnetic field around a wire carrying an electric current			
What a solenoid and an electromagnet are			
Factors that affect the strength of an electromagnet			

Key words

plotting compass   induced magnet

21.4 Plotting magnetic fields

1 The Earth has a magnetic field due to its spinning iron core.

Add arrows to the magnetic field lines of the diagram to show the direction of Earth's magnetic field.

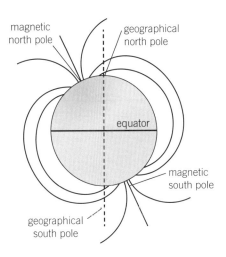

2 You can use a plotting compass to show magnetic field lines.

Add arrows to the diagram to show which direction the compass arrows will point in. The first compass has been done for you.

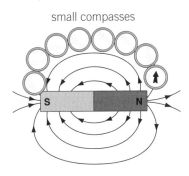

small compasses

3 Some metallic objects can be made into temporary magnets when they are put in a magnetic field. These are not permanent magnets.

What do we call these magnets? _____

Now I know:	☹	😐	☺
What the magnetic field lines of the Earth looks like			
How to use a plotting compass to visualise (see) the magnetic field of a magnet or solenoid			
What an induced magnet is			

22 Different types of waves

Key words

transverse	longitudinal	compressions	rarefactions
amplitude	wavelength	frequency	

22.1 Longitudinal and transverse waves

1   Waves oscillate (vibrate) and transfer energy from one place to another.
    There are two types of wave.

    Name the two types of wave.

    1 _____   2 _____

2   Light waves (and other electromagnetic waves) are a type of transverse wave.

    On the diagram, label:

    a   the direction of the vibrations

    b   the direction of the energy transfer

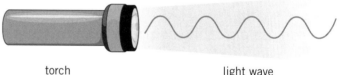

torch   light wave

3   The diagram shows a sound wave coming from a speaker (a longitudinal wave).

    On the diagram, label:

    a   the direction of the vibrations

    b   the direction of the energy transfer

4   Longitudinal waves have **compressions** and **rarefactions**.

    Label these on the longitudinal wave travelling along the slinky spring below.

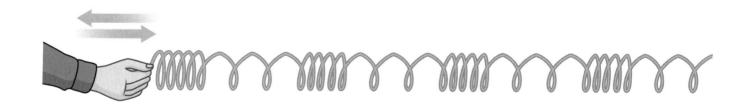

22.2 Properties of waves

1 Draw **one** line from each key word to its description.

Key word	Definition
amplitude	The number of waves passing each point per second.
frequency	The distance from a point on the wave to the same point on the next wave.
wavelength	The maximum displacement (height from highest to lowest point) from its undisturbed position.
peak	The maximum downwards displacement of the wave.
trough	The maximum upwards displacement of the wave

2 Look at the diagram of a wave. Match the letters with the key words from question 1.

A _____

B _____

C _____

D _____

E _____

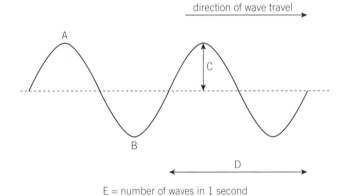

direction of wave travel

E = number of waves in 1 second

Now I know:	☹	😐	☺
The direction of energy transfer and vibration for longitudinal and transverse waves			
What rarefactions and compressions are in a longitudinal wave			
The parts of a wave			
The formula for calculating wave speed			

period (of a wave)   speed of sound

22.3 Wave measurements

1   The period of a wave is the time taken for one complete wave to pass a fixed point.

What is the formula for calculating the frequency of a wave from the period? _____

A   frequency = $\dfrac{period}{1}$

B   frequency = $\dfrac{1}{period}$

C   frequency = 1 × period

D   frequency = period × wavelength

2   The speed of a wave can be measured using the equipment shown.

Put the experiment stages in the correct order.

A	Take photos of waves moving along card.
B	Set up apparatus as shown in diagram.
C	Calculate the wavelength (by measuring the distance between 5 peaks and dividing by 4).
D	Place ruler and stopwatch on white card.
E	Change the frequency and repeat.
F	Video the waves and stopwatch. Play video back in slow motion and record the time it takes for 10 waves to pass a fixed point. Divide by 10 to get the frequency of the waves.

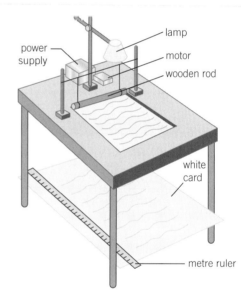

power supply, lamp, motor, wooden rod, white card, metre ruler

Correct order: ▢▢▢▢▢▢

3   Which formula can you use to calculate the speed of sound? _____

A   wave speed = frequency × wavelength   B   frequency = $\dfrac{1}{period}$ C   speed = $\dfrac{distance}{time}$

Now I know:	☹	😐	☺
How to calculate speed of sound			
How to measure the wavelength and frequency using a ripple tank			
How to calculate the frequency of a wave from the period			

23 Electromagnetic waves

Key words

electromagnetic spectrum   ionising   radio waves   microwaves   infrared
visible light   ultraviolet   X-rays   gamma rays

23.1 Electromagnetic spectrum

1   Are electromagnetic waves transverse or longitudinal waves? _____

2   Put the electromagnetic waves in order from longest wavelength to shortest.

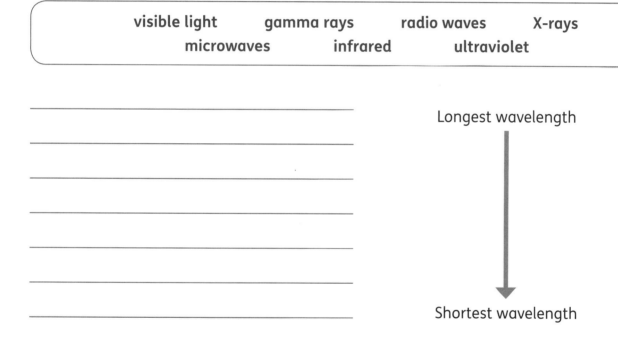

> visible light   gamma rays   radio waves   X-rays
> microwaves   infrared   ultraviolet

_____   Longest wavelength

_____

_____

_____

_____   Shortest wavelength

_____

3   Circle the electromagnetic waves that can damage living cells.

visible light   gamma rays

x-rays   microwaves

radio waves   ultraviolet

infrared

23.2 Electromagnetic waves 1

1 Draw **one** line from each electromagnetic wave to its use.

Electromagnetic wave	Use

Electromagnetic wave

- visible light
- microwaves
- radio waves
- infrared

Use

- Carrying TV signals
- Heat lamps, TV remote controls
- Cooking food
- Seeing with our eyes

2 Mobile phones have a technology called Bluetooth that lets them connect to other devices without a cable.

What type of electromagnetic waves does Bluetooth use? _____

3 Satellite communication dishes send information over large distances into space.

What sort of waves are used for communication between the dishes and satellites?

_____

4 The diagram shows a fibre optic cable.

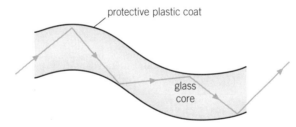

Which electromagnetic wave can be bounced along a fibre-optic cable to carry internet data?

_____

5 Which type of electromagnetic wave is involved when you barbecue food over hot charcoal?

_____

23.3 Electromagnetic waves 2

1 Draw **one** line to match each electromagnetic wave to its use.

Electromagnetic wave

| gamma rays |
| ultraviolet |
| X-rays |

Use

| Seeing inside the body |
| Killing cancer cells |
| Sun lamps |

2 Which electromagnetic wave is absorbed by security markings (like the ones used on paper money or government identification documents) and then emitted as visible light?

_____

3 X-rays are a type of ionising radiation.

People who work with X-ray equipment stand behind a special wall containing lead.

What could the X-rays do to their cells without this protection?

_____

4 What are gamma rays used for during the production of medical equipment?

_____

Now I know:	☹	😐	☺
Be able to put waves of the electromagnetic spectrum in the right order			
Know the uses of each group of the electromagnetic spectrum			
Know which of the groups of waves are dangerous			

Key words

| density | internal energy | pressure | states of matter | latent heat |

23.4 Density

1   Density tells us how much mass a substance has in a certain amount of space.

Which of these units can be used to measure density? Tick **one** box.

m/s² ☐   kg/m² ☐   kg/m³ ☐   kg ☐

2   Which of these is the formula for calculating density? _____

   A   density = mass × volume   B   density = $\dfrac{mass}{volume}$

   C   density = $\dfrac{volume}{mass}$ D   density = height × length × depth

3   The diagram shows equipment you can use to measure the density of a pebble.

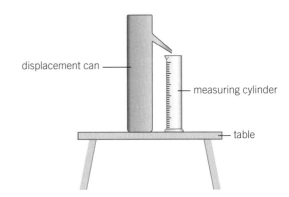

displacement can — measuring cylinder — table

Put the experiment stages in the correct order.

A	Fill a displacement can with water until water comes out of the spout. Leave it to stop dripping.
B	Drop the irregular object into the can. Catch the water that comes out of the spout in your measuring cylinder.
C	Measure the mass of your object in g.
D	Place a measuring cylinder underneath the spout.
E	Using the mass of the object (in g) and the volume of water (1 ml = 1 cm³) calculate the density of the object.

Correct order: ☐☐☐☐☐

23.5 Kinetic theory of matter

1 Draw **one** line between each state of matter to the correct particle diagram and description.

State of matter	Diagram	Description

State of matter

solid

liquid

gas

Diagram

X

Y

Z

Description

Particles are in contact with each other and can move randomly

Particles much further apart and move randomly at fast speeds

Particles vibrate in fixed positions

2 What is the name given to the energy stored inside a substance? _____

3 The particles in a gas have a lot of energy. They collide with the sides of their container and exert a force. This force is called the gas pressure.

How would increasing the temperature of the gas change the pressure?

_____

23.6 Changes of state

1 Complete the table to name the changes of state in the diagram.

Change of state	Label on diagram
Freezing	
Sublimation	
Melting	
Condensation	
Condensation	
Vaporisation (or boiling or evaporation)	

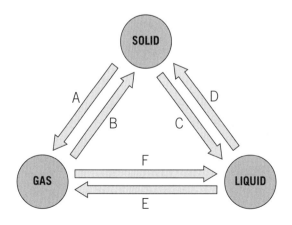

2 A teacher boils 100 g of water until all of the water (liquid) turns into a gas.

Will the mass of the gas (the steam) be:

Greater than 100 g (increased) ☐

100 g (the same) ☐

Less than 100 g (decreased) ☐

3 A scientist heated a chemical until it turned into a gas.
The scientist took the temperature every minute and plotted the results on a graph.

a Complete the table to show which statement refers to each part of the graph.

Statement	Part of the graph
The chemical is changing state from solid to liquid.	
The chemical is a gas.	
The chemical is a liquid.	
The chemical is changing state from a liquid to gas.	

b Which two parts of the graph show the temperature remaining the same due to latent heat?

_____ and _____

Now I know:	☹	😐	☺
How to calculate the density of an object			
The formula and units for density			
How particles are arranged in solids, liquids and gases			
What gas pressure is and how it is changed by temperature			
The names of changes between the states of matter			
What happens to mass and temperature during changes of state			

Component 6: Exam-style questions

1. Electric current is the flow of electrical charge.

   a   Does a circuit have to be complete or incomplete for current to flow through it?

   Circle the correct word. **[1 mark]**

   Complete   Incomplete

   b   Many factors can affect the flow of charge.

   Are the following statements about increasing the current are true or false?

   Circle **one** answer in each row. **[2 marks]**

Factor	Circle **one** answer for each row.	
Increasing the voltage across a component, increases the current flowing through it.	True	False
Decreasing the resistance of a component decreases the current flowing through it.	True	False

   c   There are two types of current. One is called alternating current (a.c.).
       What is the other one called? **[1 mark]**

       .... current

   d   Mains electricity is an a.c. supply. In the UK, what is the voltage?

   Circle **one** answer **[1 mark]**

   30 V   130 V   230 V

2. Fuses are used for our safety. If too much current passes through the fuse,
   the fuse will melt and break the circuit.

   If a dishwasher has a maximum current of 10 A, should the fuse be 9 A or 13 A? **[1 mark]**

   ....

3. The table below shows the power ratings for some common household appliances.

Appliance	Power rating in kilowatts (kW)
Refrigerator	0.2
Tumble dryer	2.5
Mobile phone charger	0.01
Iron	2.8

a Which of the appliances is the most powerful? [1 mark]

....

b The mobile phone charger is switched on for 3 hours.

Use the equation below to calculate the energy it transfers. [1 mark]

Energy in kilowatt-hours (kWh) = power in kilowatts (kW) × time in hours (h)

.... kilowatt-hours of energy

4. Magnetism is an example of a force.

When you bring two magnets close together, they will attract or repel.

a What happens when the north poles of two magnets are brought close together? [1 mark]

....

b What happens when the north poles of one magnet and the south pole of another magnet are brought close together? [1 mark]

....

c Is magnetism a contact or a non-contact force? [1 mark]

....

5. An electromagnet is a special kind of magnet.
It is made up of a long coil of wire, called a solenoid, around an iron core.

If you increase the number of coils in the solenoid,
what happens to the strength of the magnetic field?

Tick **one** box.

Strength will increase ☐

Strength will decrease ☐

There will be no change ☐ [1 mark]

6. Complete the following paragraph about electrical circuits using the words in the box. **[4 marks]**

current	ammeter	resistance	voltage

If you want to measure the current in a circuit you should use a ....

If you want to measure the .... you should use a voltmeter.

Cells and batteries provide the .... in a circuit.

The more components there are in a circuit, the higher the .... will be.

7. Electromagnetic waves exist on a continuous spectrum

   a   Decide if the following statements are true or false.   **[4 marks]**

   Circle **one** answer in each row.

Factor	Circle **one** answer for each row.	
Red light has a shorter wavelength than violet light.	True	False
X-rays are used for looking at human bones.	True	False
Humans can see gamma rays just using their eyes.	True	False
Infrared cameras help us see animals in the dark.	True	False

   b   Some waves on the electromagnetic spectrum are dangerous.

   Why must medical technicians monitor the amount of gamma
   rays they are exposed to?   **[1 mark]**

   ....

8. Waves can be either transverse or longitudinal.

   a   Draw **one** line to match each type of wave to its example.   **[1 mark]**

   Type of wave   **Example**

   | transverse | | sound wave |

   | longitudinal | | light wave |

b Waves transfer energy.

Draw and label an arrow on this transverse wave to show the direction of energy transfer. **[1 mark]**

direction of oscillation

c Draw and label another arrow on the transverse wave to show the amplitude of the wave. **[1 mark]**

Component 6: Exam-style questions (Trilogy)

01 Resistance is the measure of how difficult it is for current to flow through a component.

01.1 Give the equation for resistance that links potential difference (voltage) and current. **[1 mark]**

01.2 Using the equation you have just written, calculate the resistance of a 15 V light bulb with a current of 5 A flowing through it. **[2 marks]**

____

02 **Figure 1** shows some different electrical components.

Figure 1

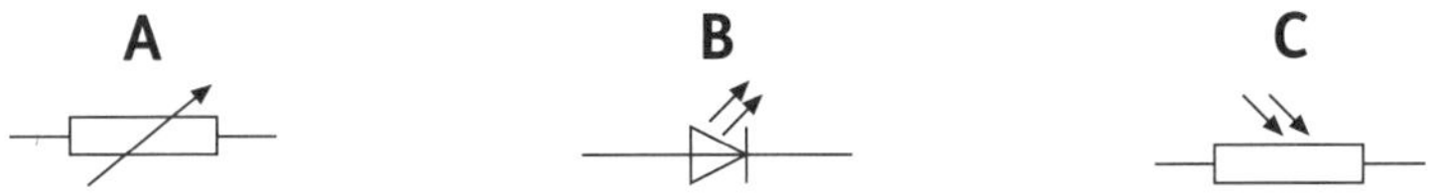

02.1 Which component is a variable resistor? **[1 mark]**

Tick **one** box.

A ☐

B ☐

C ☐

02.2 In which component will the resistance change when light is shone on it? **[1 mark]**

Tick **one** box.

A ☐

B ☐

C ☐

02.3 **Figure 2** shows 4 different ways of arranging resistors in a circuit.

Figure 2

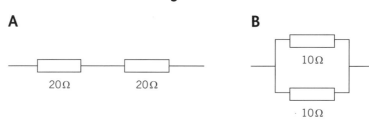

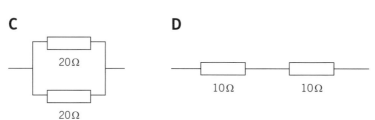

Which **two** circuits in **Figure 2** are parallel? [2 marks]

_____

02.4 Describe the difference between a series and a parallel circuit. [2 marks]

_____

_____

02.5 Which of the circuits would have the highest resistance? [2 marks]
Explain why.

_____

_____

03 The power of an appliance is the energy transferred per second.

03.1 Give the equation for power that links energy and time. [1 mark]

03.2 We can calculate the power of an appliance if we know the potential difference and the current.

Give the equation for power that links potential difference and current. [1 mark]

03.3 If an electric hairdryer works on a potential difference of 230 V, and a current of 2 A flows through it.

What is the power of the hairdryer? **[1 mark]**

Tick **one** box.

232 W ☐

460 W ☐

115 W ☐

04 The National Grid distributes electricity from power stations to homes and businesses where it is needed.

04.1 Transformers are an important part of the National Grid.

Describe what a transformer does. **[1 mark]**

_____

_____

04.2 Explain why it is more efficient to transfer energy using higher voltages. **[3 marks]**

_____

_____

_____

05 Use the correct answer from the box to complete the sentence. **[1 mark]**

| decreases | increases | stays the same |

As the distance from the magnet increases, the strength

of the magnetic field _____.

06 **Figure 3** shows a rectangular magnet, called a bar magnet.

Figure 3

06.1 Are the two magnets attracted or repelled?

_____

06.2 A bar magnet is a permanent magnet.

A bar magnet can induce magnetism in some materials.

Name **one** material in which magnetism can be induced. **[1 mark]**

_____

06.3 Give an example of where we induced magnets are used. **[1 mark]**

_____

07 Describe the difference between a transverse and a longitudinal wave.

Include 'oscillations' and 'transfer energy' in your answer. **[2 marks]**

_____

_____

_____

08 Calculate the speed of a wave that has a frequency of 200 Hz and a wavelength of 2 m.

Include the correct units with your answer. **[2 marks]**

_____

09 Water can exist as ice, water or steam.

09.1 Which form of water is the densest? **[1 mark]**

_____

09.2 Which of the following is a unit of density? **[1 mark]**

Tick **one** box.

kg ☐

kg/m ☐

kg/m^2 ☐

kg/m^3 ☐

09.3 Which of the following has the most internal energy? **[1 mark]**

Tick **one** box.

1 kg of ice ☐

1 kg of water ☐

1 kg of steam ☐

09.4 When ice is gently warmed, it turns to water (from a solid to a liquid).

Describe what happens to the water particles as the water changes state. **[3 marks]**

_____

_____

_____

Answers

1.1

1   Nucleus – where the genetic material (DNA) is kept. It controls what the cell does.

Cell membrane – lets substances pass in and out of the cells.

Cytoplasm – the 'filling' of the cell where the chemical reactions happen.

2   Sperm cell: any **one** from: tail for swimming to travel large distances; lots of mitochondria to release energy as swimming a long way requires lots of energy; head section contains chemicals to break down the outside of the egg.

Muscle cell: able to contract (get shorter) to pull the bones around and move the body.

1.2

1   a   From top: nucleus; cytoplasm; cell membrane.

b   Total magnification = eyepiece magnification × objective lens magnification

$$= 10 \times 100 = \times 1000$$

1.3

1   From left to right: cells, tissues, organs, organ systems.

2   Tissues: stomach lining cells; muscle cells. Organs: liver; small intestine; heart; stomach. Organ systems: digestive system; circulatory system

3   From left to right: Circulatory system – carries blood around the body (the blood carries oxygen, carbon dioxide, nutrients, and waste products around the body). Digestive system – digests (breaks down) food into the nutrients that our bodies need to live. Nervous system – carries messages around the body and co-ordinates many functions of the body.

1.4

1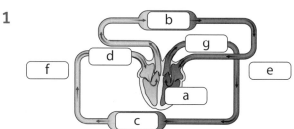

2   a   Carries oxygen around the body

b   White blood cell – fights infection, ingests pathogens, and produces antibodies.

c   Platelets – involved in clotting of blood

d   Plasma

1.5

1   Clockwise ↺ from top-left: mouth; gullet/oesophagus; stomach; pancreas; large intestine; anus; small intestine; gall bladder; liver

2   Mouth: food is chewed and mixed with saliva → Stomach: food is mixed up, acid is added here, and digestion of protein starts → Small intestine: most digestion happens here and nutrients are absorbed into the bloodstream → Large intestine: water is absorbed here → Anus: the indigestible waste (faeces) leaves the body

3   Mouth – Saliva – Contains enzymes. Lubricates food down the oesophagus

Stomach – Acid – Helps digest proteins and kill bacteria

Liver – Bile – Emulsifies fats

Pancreas – Enzymes – Help break down food in digestion

1.6

1   a   Animal cell – from top to bottom: cell membrane; ribosomes; mitochondria; cytoplasm; nucleus

Plant cell – from top to bottom: nucleus; chloroplasts; vacuole; cytoplasm; mitochondria; cell wall; ribosomes; cell membrane

b   Any **two** from: nucleus, cell membrane, cytoplasm, ribosomes, mitochondria.

c   Any **two** from: Plant cells have a cell wall (animal cells do not); plant cells have chloroplasts (animal cells do not); plant cells have a permanent vacuole (animal cells do not).

2   Cell wall – Cellulose structure

Mitochondria – Transfer energy to move minerals into the cell

Permanent vacuole – Full of sap

Root hair – Large surface area

1.7

1   Low concentration ⟵ high concentration

2   a   The dark particles are the air particles. The light particles are the perfume particles.

In diagram 1, when the assistant drops the perfume the perfume particles are all in one place.

In diagrams 2 and 3, the particles are beginning to spread out (to diffuse) from an area of high concentration to an area of low concentration (along a concentration gradient).

In diagram 4, the concentration of particles is the same (equal) and diffusion is complete.

b   The process in which cells move a substance from an area of low concentration to an area of high concentration (the opposite way to diffusion). Active transport requires energy.

1.8

1   a   Artery – Z – thick wall

Vein – Y – thin wall

Capillary – X – one cell thick wall

b   Veins

c   Arteries

d   So diffusion can happen through the capillary walls, and white blood cells can squeeze out into surrounding tissues.

2   a   Fatty deposits build up in the arteries.

b   If the arteries to the heart are blocked you have a heart attack (cardiac arrest).

1.9

1   Carbohydrases break down carbohydrates to make simple sugars like glucose.

Lipases break down fats and oils to make fatty acids and glycerol.

2   a   The enzyme has not been used up at the end of the reaction (so it can be used again).

b   If the enzyme changes shape it won't work any more.

2.1

1   The lungs

2   a   glucose + oxygen → carbon dioxide + water + energy

b   From top to bottom: oxygen; carbon dioxide; glucose.

3   Any **two** from: Building up large molecules from smaller ones; for muscles to contract; to keep your body at a constant temperature.

2.2

1   Carbohydrates – starchy food like potatoes and cereals, or sweet food like fruit – main source of energy

Lipids (fats and oils) – red meats, butter, and cheese – store energy and keep you warm

Proteins – meat, fish, eggs, beans – growth and repair

Vitamins and minerals – fruit and

vegetables – small amounts are needed to help you grow and function normally

Water – drinks (juice/water) – cells and body fluids need this to prevent dehydration

Fibre – cereals, fruit, and vegetables – help food move through the gut

2 a It is unhealthy to be overweight because this can put extra strain on the heart because it has to work harder. Overweight people are more at risk of type-2 diabetes and some types of cancer.

   b It is unhealthy to be underweight because it can be harder to fight off disease. Underweight people can lack energy and feel tired. If their diet is poor they might lack minerals and vitamins.

2.3

1 Smoking – negative. It can cause cancer and heart disease.

   Alcohol – negative. It can damage the liver; alcohol can affect the brain (this is why you can't drink and drive).

   Exercise – positive. It can make your heart stronger; makes your muscles stronger; helps you lose weight (lose excess fat).

   Eating a lot of energy-rich food – negative. It can increase your percentage of body fat (causing you to put on weight).

2 a Passive smoking

   b Passive smoking can cause health problems like bronchitis and lung disease (smoking-associated problems through breathing in second-hand smoke).

3 Being overweight

2.4

1 a Feel your pulse in your wrist and count the beats in one minute.

   b The recovery time for this person is 7 minutes. (This is the time it takes to return to the resting rate.)

   c Your pulse rate tells us how fast your heart is beating. It can be used to tell how fit you are or if you have a medical problem.

2.5

1 Lactic acid

2 a The brewing industry – alcohol.
Bread making – carbon dioxide (to make the bread rise).

   b The gas given off is carbon dioxide. We can work this out because it should turn limewater a cloudy white colour.

2.6

1 Any **three** from: diet; your fitness level; your weight; how much alcohol you drink; if you smoke; how much sun you are exposed to.

2 Row 1 – positive – as one variable increases, the other increases.
Row 2 – none – there is no link.
Row 3 – negative – as one variable increases, the other decreases.

3.1

1 Stomach acid – helps break down pathogens. Hairs and mucus in nose and throat – trap dirt and pathogens. Waterproof skin – stops pathogens getting inside the body. White blood cells – ingest pathogens that get inside the body, and produce antibodies.

2 Bacteria: microscopic cells, cause disease, produce toxins, treated with antibiotics.
Viruses: extremely small, reproduce inside a living cell, need a host cell, cause disease.

3.2

1 From top: white blood cells; pathogen; immune; antibodies.

2 A healthy person is injected with weakened pathogen (for example, part of the flu virus). Their body will produce antibodies that help the white cells fight the infection.

Antibodies that are made stay in the blood. The body remembers how to make the antibodies. When the body meets the pathogen again, it knows how to fight it (the person is immune to the pathogen).

3.3

1 a Syphilis is treated with an antibiotic.
  b Only bacterial infections can be treated with an antibiotic. Antibiotics will not work on flu because it is caused by a virus.

2 From top: side-effects; addiction; withdrawal symptoms.

3 antibiotic

3.4

1 a A is the most effective because it has the biggest area where it is stopping the bacteria from growing.
  b The zone of inhibition.
  c A ruler or squared paper.
  d To kill any bacteria (so we only transfer the ones we intend to).

2 Disinfectant

3.5

1 Bacteria usually reproduce by splitting in two. This means they reproduce very quickly as their population doubles every division.

   Viruses reproduce by taking over the host cell and getting it to make new copies of the virus. All viruses do this – they cannot reproduce on their own.

2 a Number of bacteria: (10,) 20, 40, 80, 160, 320, 640, 1280, 2560, 5120
  b Final population $= 25 \times 2^9$
         $= 25 \times 512$
         $= 12\,800$ bacteria present

3.6

1 Air – Breathing in droplets that somebody has sneezed out – On a plane, if one person sneezes droplets containing pathogens into the air, other people will breathe them in and become ill

Direct contact – Touching someone who is ill or something that has pathogens on it. – Sexually transmitted diseases, or touching contaminated door handles and furniture

Food – Disease-causing bacteria are present in food – Eating raw chicken that might contain *Salmonella* bacteria

Water – Untreated water can contain bacteria or viruses from human or animal sewage – Diseases like cholera are caught by drinking dirty water

2 Colds and influenza: catching sneezes in a tissue; washing hands

   Food poisoning: cooking food thoroughly; good food hygiene when preparing and cooking food

   Sexually transmitted diseases: use of a condom

   Malaria (spread through mosquito bites): mosquito nets and insect repellent to keep the insects away

   Waterborne diseases like cholera: boil or treat the water before using it

3.7

1 From top: true, true, false, true.
2 1. Drug designed on computer or isolated from nature
   2. Laboratory (in vitro) testing
   3. Testing on animals
   4. Small-scale tests on people
   5. Small-scale testing with ill people
   6. Large-scale testing on lots of people

4.1

1 A, D, F
2 A, B, D

4.2

1 a Student – 0.23 s, Friend 1 – 0.3 s, Friend 2 – 0.33 s
  b The student
  c If you repeat an experiment several times you can take an average, spot anomalous results, and check your answers are repeatable.

2 Caffeine **or** age (being younger)

3 Any **one** from: alcohol, some illegal drugs, being tired, age (being older), distractions (for example, using a phone while driving).

4.3

1 Clockwise ⟲ from top-right: pituitary gland, adrenal gland, ovary (female), testis (male), pancreas, thyroid gland.

2 a They are secreted (released) into the bloodstream and carried around the body in the circulatory system.

  b Target organs

3 Day 1 – B, F. Day 7 – A. Day 14 – D, E. Day 21 – C.

4.4

1 Type of contraception. The pill.

  How do you take this type of contraception? Swallow it – take a tablet every day.

  How does it work? It stops the egg maturing and being released so a woman can't get pregnant.

2 B

4.5

1 Clockwise ⟲ from top left: B, D, A, C.

2 a The second half of the cycle, after day 14 (days 14–21 are the most likely).

  b Because the egg cell won't have been released.

3 a The condom catches the sperm so it can't swim away towards an egg cell.

  b Any **one** from: Condoms also prevent the spread of sexually transmitted diseases; cheap; easily available; easy to use.

4.6

1 Any **two** from: Blood glucose level; body temperature; amount of water in your blood.

2 a Row 1 – blood glucose level will start to go up as you digest the food and absorb the sugar.

  Row 2 – blood glucose level will go down as glucose is removed from the blood.

Row 3 – blood glucose level will drop as respiration will happen at a faster rate.

  b The blood glucose level would rise (go up). This would be bad for the person because it can cause damage to your organs.

Component 1: Exam-style questions

1 a Nucleus [1]

  b Red blood cell [1]

  c Contain haemoglobin that binds oxygen [1] **or** has no nucleus to make more space for oxygen [1]

2 From top: tissue [1], heart [1], circulatory system [1]

3 a From top: lungs [1], liver [1], intestines [1]

  b Smoking cigarettes – lung cancer. [1]

    Drinking large amounts of alcohol – liver damage. [1]

    Eating a diet with more energy in – becoming overweight (obese). [1]

  c Your lungs can get bigger. [1] Your BMI is likely to be lower. [1]

4 a They travel down nerves, and don't have to go to the brain [1]

  b Knee-jerk reaction [1] **or** response to bright light [1] **or** response to dim light [1]

5 a Protein [1]

  b Carbohydrates [1]

  c 18-year old-males [1]

  d They are still growing / more active. [1]

6 a Bacteria [1], Viruses [1]

  b White blood cells [1]

  c You are injected with inactive or dead pathogens [1]

  d Antibodies [1]

7 a Hormones [1], blood [1], period [1]

  b From top: true [1], false [1], false [1]

  c Advantages – **one** from: convenient; reliable; safe. [1]

    Disadvantages – **one** from: doesn't stop STDs; need to remember to take pill. [1]

Component 1: Exam-style questions (Trilogy)

01   cell wall [1], chloroplasts [1], permanent vacuole [1]

02.1 Any **two** from: concentration gradient [1], temperature [1], surface area [1]

02.2 Active transport [1]

02.3 Nutrients / minerals [1]

02.4 Mitochondria [1]

03.1 Enzyme [1]

03.2 Speeds it up / increases the rate [1]

04.1 Heart [1], fat [1], blood [1], oxygen [1], correlation [1].

04.2 Any **one** from: increase fitness / exercise level; maintain a healthy weight. [1]

04.3 Bypass surgery – damaged arteries replaced with vessels from other parts of the body.

Statins – Drugs are given to reduce the rate of fatty deposits in blood vessels.

Stents – A metal tube is inserted in a blood vessel to hold it open. [All correct for 2 marks; 1 correct for 1 mark]

05.1 Lactic acid [1]

05.2 It causes a stitch / cramp / pain [1]

05.3 Oxygen debt [1]

05.4 Fermentation [1]

06.1 Hand washing [1], wearing a face mask [1]

06.2 X: 10×2^3 [1] = 80 cells [1]
      Y: 15×2^2 [1] = 60 cells [1]

06.3 X [1]

06.4 Any **two** from: effective [1], safe [1], stable [1], easy to take [1].

07.1 28 [1]

07.2 Follicle stimulating hormone [1], oestrogen [1]

08.1 Insulin [1]

08.2 Pancreas [1]

08.3 They ate a meal. [1]

08.4 Person 1 [1]

5.1

1 a A producer is an organism that makes its own food using energy from the sun. A consumer is an organism that eats (consumes) other animals or plants to survive.

   b Producers – grass, dandelion, tree
      Consumer – slug, bird, greenfly, cow

2 a carbon dioxide + water $\xrightarrow{\text{light}}$ glucose + oxygen

   b In the leaves (of a plant)

   c Chlorophyll

   d Chloroplasts

5.2

1 Habitat – where an organism lives.
   Organism – a living thing.
   Adaptation – A special feature that helps an organism to survive where it lives.

2 a Covered in spines.

   b Large feet – stops them sinking into the snow. White fur – camouflage. Greasy coat – makes fur waterproof.

   c Blubber helps keep the penguin warm.

5.3

1 Ecosystem – all of the organisms and the physical conditions in an area. Population – the total number of organisms of each species in a habitat. Community – all of the populations of organisms in an ecosystem. Food chain – a diagram showing the feeding relationships in a community (also shows transfer of energy)

2

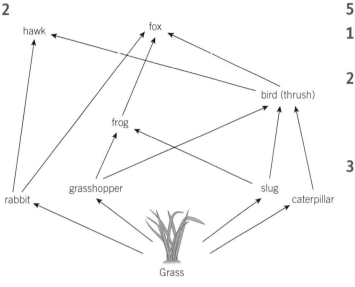

5.4

1 Materials (like carbon) can be recycled. If they weren't recycled we would run out of materials to make new plants and animals out of. If dead things didn't decay the Earth would be covered in dead plants and animals.

2 a Bacteria, worms, and fungi

   b Carbon dioxide

   c Use it for growing plants in

5.5

1 With no bees there would be no pollination and so the plants would not be able to produce seeds. Eventually they would become extinct.

2 As the number of hares increases, the population of lynx will increase as well. When the population of hares goes down, the population of lynx will go down as well – this is how they are interdependent (the population size of the lynx depends on having enough hares to eat, and the population size of the hares depends on not being eaten by a lynx).

5.6

1 Light; carbon dioxide; temperature; amount of chlorophyll in the leaves.

2 The green part of the leaf (shown dark in the picture) would contain starch. The white part has no chlorophyll and does not photosynthesise (so there will be no starch).

3

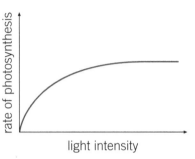

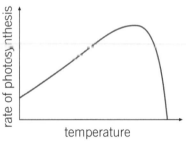

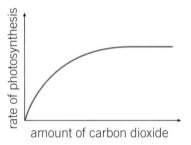

4 a A propane burner would burn fossil fuels to make carbon dioxide. Increasing the carbon dioxide will increase the rate of photosynthesis as carbon dioxide level is a limiting factor.

   b The rate of photosynthesis would be increased which would lead to the growth of his tomato plants increasing. The farmer would get bigger tomato plants and a bigger yield (crop size) of tomatoes.

5.7

1 a From top: 36, 29, 23, 14, 11.
  b Oxygen
  c The rate of production of bubbles decreases / fewer bubbles are produced every minute.
  d Light
  e LED bulbs don't give off heat. Temperature is also a limiting factor for photosynthesis, so heating the water with a filament bulb would affect the results.

5.8

1 a Photosynthesis.
  b Any **one** from: burning fossil fuels, decay, respiration.

6.1

1 Animals compete for: territory, mates, food.
  Plants compete for: light, nutrients/water, space.
2 Nutrients, light
3 Food, territory, mates
4 a Light   b Mates

6.2

1 Living factors: B, C, E
  Non-living factors: A, D, F
2 a Non-living
  b It would be reduced
3 a The plant populations would have decreased because the rabbits ate the plants.
  b This would cause populations of other animals to be reduced because they wouldn't have as many plants to eat.

6.3

1 a D, C, A, F, E, B
  b Do: B, C
    Don't: A, D
2 The sample taken on the footpath was sample 3. I know this because it had the fewest species (only three species found whereas sample 4 had four species, and samples 1 and 2 had 5 species) and the lowest total number / frequency of plants.

6.4

1 Land pollution: herbicide, litter, pesticides.
  Water pollution: fertilisers running off farm land; dumping untreated sewage in rivers; fertilisers entering rivers and streams.
  Air pollution: acid rain; smoke.
2 Pesticide – farmland – kill the wrong species, enter food chain, and poison humans.
  Fertiliser in a river – farmland – causes unwanted plants to grow **or** might harm animals.
  Acid rain – power stations and burning fossil fuels (for example diesel in cars) – harms plants / trees **or** kills fish and aquatic animals and plants.

6.5

1 Increase biodiversity: C, D, F
  Decreases biodiversity: A, B, E
2 a Overfishing will reduce the number of types of fish.
  b Pollution would also reduce the number of types of fish.

6.6

1 There are no more left anywhere on Earth.
2 a Green corridors will increase biodiversity.
  b This will happen because they will provide food and a habitat for different species. They also provide shelter for animals, allowing them to rest when moving between areas.
3 a A breeding programme takes animals that are endangered and breeds them (and may introduce them to the wild)
  b Maintaining genetic diversity / maintaining a large enough population; Getting the animals to survive in the wild after being reared in captivity.

7.1

1 Nucleus

2 DNA – a long molecule containing the information needed to make an organism. Chromosomes – long tangled strands of DNA, organised in pairs. Genes – short sections of DNA that carry a specific piece of information.

3 **a** 23   **b** 46   **c** 2 (or 1 pair)   **d** male

7.2

1 Sexual reproduction: needs two parents; the offspring contains DNA from 2 parents; likely to show variation; the offspring is different from both parents.

Asexual reproduction: the offspring contains DNA from 1 parent; the offspring is genetically identical to its parent; unlikely to show variation; only 1 parent needed.

2 Any **one** from: pollen and ovule in a plant; sperm and egg in an animal.

3 A clone is genetically identical to its parent.

4 **a** Asexual reproduction

   b The offspring would be identical to the parent.

7.3

1 Inherited: blonde hair, detached earlobes, eye colour.

Environmental: tattoo, scar.

2 **a**

b A

c There is a positive correlation between height and shoe size.

7.4

1 Natural selection

2 B

3 **a** C, B, D, A

   b It got darker (covered in soot)

   c There is now less pollution, so the tree bark is lighter in colour, and black moths are easier for birds to spot and eat.

4 True: D, E

   False: A, B, C

7.5

1 D, B, C, E, A

2 Any **two** from: larger fruit; bigger crop of fruit (bigger yield); better taste; resistance to disease or drought.

3 In only one generation of breeding the farmer would only see small changes. It takes many generations to get a big change and to make sure the plant only has the genes the farmer wants.

7.6

1 Genes, quick; characteristics / genetic traits, slow; different

2 Benefit: any **one** from: can change just one feature of an animal or plant; it is quick – it only takes a single generation; you can control what characteristics you want the new organism to have.

Risk: any **one** from: the modified organism might breed with wild plants or unmodified animals and transfer modified genes to the offspring; people worry about the long-term effects of eating modified food; some people are ethically opposed to it.

7.7

1 Gene – these control the different characteristics of an organism.

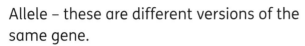

Allele – these are different versions of the same gene.

Dominant – a gene that only needs one copy of an allele for the characteristic to be expressed (shown) in the organism.

Recessive – a gene that needs two copies of the same allele for the characteristic to be expressed (shown) in the organism.

2   BB – Brown – Homozygous

    Bb – Brown – Heterozygous

    bb – Blonde – Homozygous

3   The genotype is the combination of alleles (versions of the same gene) in an organism.

    The phenotype is the observable (can see it) characteristic the organism displays (for example, hair colour).

7.8

1 a   female   b   male

2 a

	F	f
F	**FF**	**Ff**
f	**Ff**	**ff**

  b   FF – 1/4 – 25%

      Ff – 2/4 – 50%

      ff – 1/4 – 25%

  c   25% (has genotype ff)

  d   75% (has genotype FF or Ff)

Component 2: Exam-style questions

1 a   photosynthesis [1]

  b   oxygen [1]

2   Long trunk – reach food in high branches and on the ground.

    Tusks – strip bark from trees for food

    Large ears – flap to keep cool in hot weather. [All correct for 2 marks; 1 correct for 1 mark]

3 a   The frog eats the grasshopper. [1]

  b   Grass [1]

  c   Arrow from grasshopper to shrew [1]; arrow from shrew to snake [1]; arrow from shrew to hawk [1].

  d   Competing [1]

4 a   Sun [1]

  b   Decay [1]

  c   Interdependence [1]

5   Space [1]

6   Air temperature [1], increased rainfall [1]

7   Sulfur dioxide [1]

8   Cars driving – produces gas that causes acid rain; spraying herbicide – pollution in streams near the field; local picnic spot – litter is dropped [All correct for 2 marks; two correct for 1]

9   (Gene,) chromosome [1], nucleus [1], cell [1]

10 Evolution [1], natural selection [1], more [1]

11 a   Female [1]

   b   Male [1]

12 Farmers can breed animals like cows to have bigger muscles (more meat). [1]

Component 2: Exam-style questions (Trilogy)

01.1   Respiration – B, decay – C, photosynthesis – A, fossil fuel formation – D [All correct for 3 marks; 2 correct for 2 marks; 1 correct for 1 mark]

01.2   When organisms die, decomposers break down remains. [1] This releases carbon dioxide into the atmosphere. [1]

02.1   The number of different species of living organism in an area [1]

02.2   Burning fossil fuels - acid rain; using pesticides - pollutes local waterways; digging up peat - habitat destruction; increasing the number of houses - creates more rubbish [All correct for 3 marks; 2 correct for 2 marks; 1 correct for 1 mark]

02.3   Create a stable / healthy population of a species [1] to reintroduce back into their natural habitat. [1]

03 Dominant [1]

04 31 [1]

05 Choose one horse that is fast and one that has stamina. [1] Breed horses together. [1] From offspring, choose offspring with speed and stamina. [1] Breed horses together. [1] Eventually have a group of fast horses with good stamina. [1]

06.1 Seal [1]

06.2 The population of squid will increase [1] because there is more food. [1]

06.3 Fish population starts higher than seals [1].
Fish population rises after seal population falls. [1]
Fish population falls as seal population rises. [1]

06.4 Any **one** from: territory [1], mates [1]

06.5 Any **one** from: biodiversity decreases [1], ecosystem becomes less stable [1]

07.1 Faster / greater [1]

07.2 [1 mark for 2 points plotted, 2 marks for all plotted]

07.3 Enzymes are damaged. [1]
Photosynthesis no longer happens. [1]

07.4 Any **one** from: light intensity [1]; concentration of carbon dioxide [1]; amount of chlorophyll [1]

07.5 Chloroplast [1]

08.1

XX [1]	XY [1]
XX [1]	XY [1]

08.2 50% **or** 2 in 4 **or** ½ [1]

08.3 50% **or** 2 in 4 **or** ½ [1]

08.4 Any **two** from: different genes [1]; different combination of alleles [1]; different environmental effects

8.1

1 Atoms

2 a Elements only have one type (kind) of atom.

b (Numbers added above main columns, in order: 1, 2, 3, 4, 5, 6, 7, 0)

c (All elements to the left of the stepped line)

d 7   **e** 1   **f** Non-metal

8.2

1 a Group 1   **b** Group 7

2 Hydrogen

3 a Increases from top to bottom

b Increases from bottom to top

8.3

1 B

2 Elements: A, D   Compounds: B, C

3 a Sodium + oxygen → sodium oxide

b Magnesium + oxygen → magnesium oxide

c Iron + sulfur → iron sulfide

4 a From top: oxide, sulfide, chloride, bromide, sulfate, nitrate.

b From top: iron sulfate; magnesium chloride; lithium bromide; potassium nitrate

8.4

1 Clockwise ↻ from top-left: electron, proton, neutron, nucleus. (Proton and neutron can be either way round.)

2 Electron, –1, very small
Neutron, 0, 1
Proton, +1, 1

3 Mg has 12 protons and 12 neutrons.
F has 9 protons and 10 neutrons.
Ne has 7 protons and 7 neutrons.

4 Isotopes have different numbers of neutrons (the same number of protons).

8.5

1

2   Sodium: 2,8,1

Oxygen: 2,6

Chlorine: 2,8,7

Lithium: 2,1

Potassium: 2,8,8,1

3   The number of electrons in the outer shell of an element is the same as the group number.

8.6

1   Left side

2   **Two** from: conduct electricity, are shiny, are flexible

3   a   ions

b   2+

c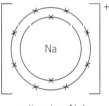

sodium ion, Na$^+$
2,8

4   Because the atoms get bigger and it is easier for them to lose their outer electron.

8.7

1   Right

2   **Two** from: usually brittle, good insulators, dull

3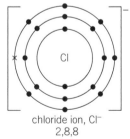

chloride ion, Cl$^-$
2,8,8

4   Top of group 7

5   Potassium chloride and bromine

Sodium bromide and iodine

Magnesium fluoride and bromine

9.1

1   Solids – X – Particles are touching and arranged in a regular pattern; they are fixed in place and cannot move about, only vibrate.

Liquids – Z – Particles are touching but are NOT arranged in a regular pattern; they are able to move about and change place.

Gases – Y – The particles are not touching; there is space between them and they move about in all directions.

2   a   Melting

b   Condensation

c   Freezing

d   Evaporation/boiling

3   The forces between particles in a metal must be strong because most metals have high melting points.

The forces between particles in a non-metal must be weak because most non-metals have low melting points.

9.2

1   a   B

b   It contains particles of several different compounds or elements.

2   Clockwise ⟲ from top-right: sand (residue), water (filtrate), funnel, filter paper.

3   It evaporates.

4   a   Distillation   c   Filtration

b   Crystallisation   d   Filtration

9.3

1   Solvent – the liquid the substance is dissolved in;

Solute – the substance that is dissolved;

Solvent front – where the liquid has moved to up the filter paper;

Chromatogram – the piece of paper left (the result) of a chromatography experiment;

Solution – the solute dissolved in the solvent.

2   The pencil will not dissolve in the solvent and will not move up the filter paper or separate.

3   Pink

9.4

1   a   Diamond (X); graphite (Y)

b X – any **three** from: hard, strong, high melting point, doesn't conduct electricity

Y – soft, slippery, conducts electricity

2 Diamond is very strong and hard-wearing.

3 It is slippery.

9.5

1 a

b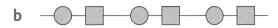

2 Advantage: A, C, D

Disadvantage: B

3 They are not biodegradable.

9.6

1 C

2 a Substance B

b This substance will freeze at one temperature.

3 Any **one** from: fuels, cleaning agents, paints, medicines, alloys, fertilisers, foods.

9.7

1 The solution with the highest concentration is B. I can tell because it has the most solute (the chemical being dissolved) in the solvent (liquid it is dissolved in).

2 concentration $(g/dm^3) = 50 \div 2 = 25 \, g/dm^3$

3 Mass of solute in $g = 50 \times 4 = 200 \, g$

9.8

1 a Carbon dioxide, oxygen, methane

b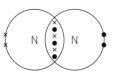

2 The electrical conductivity as a solid or liquid would be **poor**; the melting and boiling points would be **low**.

3 a E.g., diamond, graphite

b Ask your teacher to check your diagram is correct.

9.9

1 Iron oxide, copper sulfate, sodium chloride

2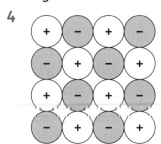

2,8   MgO   2,8

3 The electrical conductivity when melted or dissolved would be good (a bulb would light up); the melting and boiling points would be high.

4

10.1

1 a Left   **b** Solid

c

2 a High   **b** Flexible   **c** Conductors

3 It is used for water pipes because it is unreactive.

It is used for electrical cables because it is a good conductor.

4 A tough layer of aluminium oxide forms on the surface of the aluminium. This protects the aluminium from further corrosion.

10.2

1 B

2 True: B, C, D, E. False: A.

3 a Iron   **b** Carbon

c It won't rust when it is wet

10.3

1 Any **one** from: gold, silver, platinum.

2 a Ore   b Extraction
3 a Any **one** from: zinc, iron, tin, lead, copper.
   b Any **one** from: potassium, sodium, calcium, magnesium, aluminium.

10.4

1 An ore is a rock containing enough metal to be worth extracting.
2 In the ground.
3 a Any **one** from: more jobs, income to local shops, more services built like schools and hospitals.
   b Any **one** from: noise, dust, pollution, traffic.
4 a Melting down and using again to make a new product.
   b Any **two** from: to save energy; to save resources; to keep materials out of landfill; to reduce pollution and greenhouse gases.

10.5

1 a Any **one** from: silver, gold, platinum.
   b Calcium
2 From top to bottom: no – silver nitrate + gold; yes – copper + zinc sulfate; yes – magnesium chloride and zinc
3 Iron, magnesium, and calcium

10.6

1 Copper oxide, magnesium chloride, and aluminium oxide
2 Electrode
3 a Aluminium is more reactive than carbon so it wouldn't work.
   b The electricity costs a lot of money (as does the heat needed to make the process work).
   c It reacts with the oxygen to make carbon dioxide.

10.7

1 Positive electrode: anode.
   Negative electrode: cathode

2 Anode (positive) – non-metal; cathode (negative) – metal
3 a i halogen gas   ii oxygen
   b i hydrogen gas   ii metal
4 Molten sodium chloride (NaCl): chlorine at the positive; sodium metal at the negative.
   Sodium chloride solution (NaCl): chlorine at the positive; hydrogen at the negative.
   Sulfuric acid (H_2SO_4): oxygen at the positive; hydrogen at the negative.

10.8

1 If something is sustainable it means we can use it but there will be enough for us to use and for future generations.
2 There is only a certain amount of it and it will run out eventually.
3 Reduce – food waste, disposable nappies
   Reuse – clothing, plastic storage container, empty glass jar
   Recycle – empty drinks can, empty glass jar, clothing, plastic storage container

Component 3: Exam-style questions

1 X – liquid, Y – solid, Z – gas [All correct for 2 marks; 1 correct for 1 mark]
2 a −39°C [1]
   b Element [1]
   c Conduct heat well [1]
3 a Ore [1]
   b Alloy [1]
4 a Chlorine [1]
   b X – sodium; Y – sodium hydride; Z – hydrogen [All correct for 2 marks; 1 correct for 1 mark]
   c Sodium oxide [1]
5 a An element [1]
   b Right [1]
   c 7 [1]
   d 1 [1]

6 a **One** from: A mixture can be easily separated **or** in a compound the elements are joined together by chemical bonds. [1]

  b Filtration [1]

7 Red [1], yellow [1]

8 a Monomer [1]

  b Circle contains two carbon atoms on the main chain, and everything attached to them above and below. [1]

9 a Gold / platinum [1]

  b Any **one** from: zinc, iron, tin, lead [1]

  c £8.40 × 5 = £42 to extract [1]

    No, the rock is not an ore. [1]

  d Any **one** from: saves energy; saves raw resources (materials); reduces landfill. [1]

Component 3: Exam-style questions (Trilogy)

01.1 From top: +1 [1], –1 [1], neutron [1]

01.2 12 [1]

01.3 The inner shell should have 2 electrons [1]; the outer shell should have 5 electrons (giving the electronic structure 2,5). [1]

01.4 2 [1]

02 From top: ionic [1], ionic [1], covalent [1]

03.1 30 [1]

03.2 35 [1]

04.1 Strong and hard – diamond [1]; soft and slippery – graphite [1]; does not conduct electricity – diamond [1]

04.2 Each carbon atom is joined to 3 others [1] with strong bonds [1]. The atoms are arranged in layers of hexagons. [1]

04.3 6 [1]

05.1 Any **one** from: soft; low density compared to other metals; low melting point compared to other metals; (compared… is essential to gain mark); one electron in outer shell; can be cut with a knife. [1]

05.2 Lithium chloride [1]

05.3 A potassium atom is bigger than a lithium atom. [1] Therefore, it is easier for potassium to lose its outer electron. [1]

06.1 A – Copper sulfate + magnesium [1]

06.2 Magnesium sulfate [1] + copper [1]

07.1 One dot and one cross in the overlap between the circles. [1]

07.2 Ionic [1]

07.3 Giant structure [1]

08.1 Ions move about in the liquid [1]

08.2 Sodium metal – cathode; chlorine gas – anode. [1]

08.3 Hold a piece of damp blue litmus paper in the gas. [1] Chlorine would bleach the paper. [1]

09.1 Aluminium + oxygen [1]

09.2 Lower melting point [1]

09.3 At high temperatures [1] oxygen reacts with the electrode. [1]

09.4 Any **one** from: uses less energy; reduces waste in landfill; reduces amount of resources used. [1]

10.1 A [1]

10.2 C [1]

10.3 B [1]

10.4 $\frac{75}{0.3}$ [1] = 250 g/dm³ [1]

11.1

1 From the top: acids; neutral; alkalis

2 Sodium hydroxide, magnesium oxide, calcium carbonate

3 a Potassium sulfate + water

  b Magnesium chloride + water

  c Calcium chloride + water + carbon dioxide

  d Sodium sulfate + water

  e Copper sulfate + water + carbon dioxide

4 Crystallisation

11.2

1 a Hydrogen

  b Ignite with a lit splint: it should explode with a squeaky pop

2 a Magnesium sulfate + hydrogen
  b Zinc chloride + hydrogen
  c Magnesium chloride + hydrogen
  d Iron sulfate + hydrogen
3 Any **one** from: gold, silver, platinum, copper.

11.3

1 a Neutralisation
  b Carbon dioxide
  c Bubble through lime water (the lime water will turn cloudy)
2 a There would be no more bubbling/fizzing.
  b Higher (pH would be 7)
  c Removing the insoluble copper carbonate from the liquid – filtering
    Removing some of the water from the pure solution of the salt – evaporation
    Making dry crystals of the salt they produced – crystallisation

11.4

1 a acid, red
  b neutral, green
  c alkali, purple
2 a Hydrogen ion   b H$^+$(aq)
3 a Hydroxide ion   b OH$^-$ (aq)
4 a pH of 7
  b H$^+$ (aq) + OH$^-$ (aq) → H$_2$O (l)
5 A solution with pH < 7 is an acid because there are many hydrogen ions in solution.
  A solution with pH > 7 is an alkali because there are many hydroxide ions in solution.

11.5

1 From top-left: Cl, O, H$_2$O, CuCO$_3$, Zn, HCl, H$_2$SO$_4$, CO$_2$
3 a 2HCl   c 2H$_2$O
  b 2CO$_2$ d 2Mg, 2MgO
4 a CuCO$_3$ + 2HCl(l) → CuCl$_2$(aq) + CO$_2$(g) + H$_2$O(l)
  b Mg(s) + H$_2$SO$_4$(aq) → MgSO$_4$(aq) + H$_2$(g)
  c NaOH(aq) + HCl(aq) → NaCl(aq) + H$_2$O(l)

12.1

1 a Increases   b Decreases
2 From top: to the surroundings; to the system; to the surroundings; to the system

12.2

1 a slower
  b faster, more
2 Because there are more particles of acid and so (successful) collisions are more likely to occur.
3 a X – magnesium ribbon, Y – magnesium powder
  b Because the surface area is greater so (successful) collisions are more likely to occur.
4 From top: false; false; true

12.3

1 a A reaction when a solid reacts to produce a gas.
  b Down
2 B

12.4

1 Endothermic – transfers energy from surroundings so there is a temperature decrease – Y
  Exothermic – transfers energy to the surroundings so there is a temperature increase – X
2 a Activation energy   b Y
3 a A catalyst increases the rate of a reaction.
  b A catalyst would lower the activation energy.

12.5

1 A
2 g/s, cm^3/s
3 a X
  b The reaction has finished, making the same amount of products for each line.
4 2 g/s

12.6

1 Any **two** from: temperature, surface area, catalyst.

2 B

3 a 80 g/dm³ acid

 b Both reactions have finished (so the rate would be zero).

13.1

1 a Photosynthesis

 b Any **one** from: carbon dioxide dissolving in the oceans; carbon dioxide being trapped in fossil rocks and carbonates (sea shells made of calcium carbonate).

2 Y, Z, W, X

3 X – nitrogen; Y – oxygen; Z – carbon dioxide

13.2

1 Under the ground/under the sea bed.

2 Crude oil was formed from the remains of animals that lived millions of years ago.

3 a Fractional distillation

 b Arrow from bottom to top

 c Top of tower = petroleum gases and petrol. Bottom of tower = diesel and tar

13.3

1 They are made of hydrogen and carbon (and nothing else).

2 a Carbon dioxide and water

 b Carbon monoxide

3 We could test the gas by bubbling it through limewater. It should turn cloudy if carbon dioxide is present.

4 Carbon/soot

5 Carbon dioxide and water (vapour)

13.4

1 Sulfur dioxide and nitrogen dioxide

2 Acid rain reacts chemically with marble and limestone and causes weathering, meaning they break down.

3 a Carbon monoxide

 b It is poisonous/harmful

4 Global dimming

13.5

1 a The greenhouse effect

 b Carbon dioxide: burning fossil fuels. Methane: from landfill sites and rearing cattle.

2 a Increases the amount of carbon dioxide released into atmosphere.

 b Reduces the uptake / removal of carbon dioxide from the atmosphere by photosynthesis, **or** trees could be burnt, releasing carbon dioxide.

3 Any **two** from: melting of the polar ice caps; rising sea levels, more extreme weather, desert areas get bigger.

13.6

1 Cracking

2 From top: alkene, butene; alkane, ethane; alkane, pentane; alkene, ethene.

3 From top: alkane; alkene; alkene; alkane.

13.7

1 Carbon dioxide

2 a Cutting down trees; using electricity made from burning coal or gas; flying in an aeroplane.

 b 1. Walking means less carbon dioxide is emitted from burning fossil fuels such as petrol.

   2. Fewer resources are needed to grow vegetables to eat than to feed cattle.

   3. Less energy is needed to reuse products than to make new ones from scratch.

   4. Less carbon dioxide is emitted from burning fossil fuels to produce electricity.

3 Any **one** from: underground storage of carbon dioxide is expensive; it hasn't been tested; it could be unreliable; it might not be able to cope with the large amounts of carbon dioxide we emit.

14.1

1 From top: 2, 3, 4, 1, 5

2 a Clockwise ⟲ from top-left:
       Thermometer, water out, condenser,
       drinking water, cold water in,
       undrinkable water.

    b Distillation is expensive because of the
       energy required to heat the water.

14.2

1 a Correct order: D; B; F; A; C; E.

    b Sample Y.

2 pH 7

14.3

1 It would be dangerous to our health
   because it contains harmful bacteria and
   chemicals.

2 Screening – removal of large lumps like
   twigs and baby wipes.
   Sedimentation – sludge allowed to settle.
   Aerobic digestion – bacteria breaks down
   organic matter.

3 a Methane gas can be burned for energy/
       to make electricity.

    b Treated sludge can be used as fertiliser.

Component 4: Exam-style questions

1 a Nitrogen [1]

    b Photosynthesis [1]

    c Nitrogen oxides [1], sulfur dioxide [1]

    d Carbon dioxide [1]

    e The greenhouse effect [1]

2 An energy transfer to the system. [1]

3 Distillation [1]

4 a Fractional distillation [1]

    b Oxygen; carbon dioxide [1]

    c Any **one** from: carbon (soot) **or** carbon
       monoxide. [1]

    d Acid rain [1]

5 a Carbon dioxide [1]

    b Clear; cloudy [1]

    c Sulfate [1]

    d Neutralisation [1]

6 Filtration – remove solids from the water
   [1]; sterilisation – kill any microbes in the
   water. [1]

7 a Chloride [1]

    b Increased [1]; to [1]

    c Evaporation; crystallisation [1]

8 a 30°C [1]

    b Lit splint [1]

    c You will hear a pop. [1]

9 a Powdered magnesium

    b Increase the concentration of sulfuric
       acid. [1]

Component 4: Exam-style questions (Trilogy)

01.1 Screening – removes large solids.
      Sedimentation – grit and dirt allowed to
      settle out.
      Aerobic digestion – microbes break
      down organic matter in the presence
      of oxygen. [2 marks for all three right,
      1 mark for 1 or 2 right]

01.2 Oxygen [1]

02.1 Purple [1]

02.2 Potassium chloride [1]

03.1 Any **one** from: burning hydrocarbon
      fuels [1] **or** rubbish in landfill sites [1] **or**
      cows on cattle farms. [1]

03.2 Any **one** from: polar ice caps melt [1]
      – animals lose their habitat [1] **or** sea
      levels rise [1] – increase in flooding
      around the coast [1] **or** more extreme
      weather [1] – more tropical storms and
      longer periods of drought [1] **or** desert
      gets hotter and drier and grow in size. [1]

03.3 The total amount of carbon dioxide and
      other greenhouse gases made during
      the entire lifecycle of the product/event/
      service/person. [1]

04.1 Cracking [1]

04.2 Alkenes [1]

04.3 A – alkane [1]; B – alkene [1]

05   H^+ make the solution acidic.
      OH^- make the solution alkaline. [1]

06.1   W – acid [1]; X – alkali [1]; Y – neutral [1]

06.2   Acid [1]

07.1   Sodium chloride [1]

07.2   Neutralisation [1]

07.3 $H_2(g)$ [1]

07.4   2Na [1]

08.1   Salt (sodium chloride) [1]

08.2   One from: it is expensive; it produces lots of carbon dioxide. [1]

09.1   Decreases [1]; faster [1]

09.2   Sulfuric acid [1]

09.3   19 [1]

09.4   Endothermic [1]

09.5   B [1]

15.1

1   Any **three** from: chemical, kinetic, gravitational potential, thermal, elastic (or strain)

2   a   Kinetic   b   Kinetic   c   Chemical
    d   Gravitational potential
    e   Elastic (or strain)

3   a   Heating   b   Mechanically
    c   Mechanically   d   Electrically

15.2

1   Created or destroyed

2   a   Wasted   b   Useful
    c   Useful   d   Useful

3   Increase (get hotter)

4   Lubrication (oiling)

15.3

1   a   Copper   b   Highest

2   a   Felt   b   Air

3   Fill with an insulator (cavity wall insulation).

15.4

1   Renewable will never run out.
    Non-renewable will eventually run out.

2   Renewable: b, d, e. Non-renewable: a, c

3   C, A, D, B, E

15.5

1   Joules (J)

2   B

3   LED lighting – 90%

4   They waste less energy.

15.6

1   a   Carbon dioxide
    b   It would be reduced.

2   Acid rain

3   a   Carbon dioxide
    b   Dangerous (it is radioactive for millions of years)

4   B and D

16.1

1   A force is a push or a pull that acts on an object because of another object.

2   a   B and C   b   C

3   Contact: friction, air resistance, tension.
    Non-contact: gravitational force, magnetic.

4   Newtons (N)

16.2

1   Joules (J)

2   Friction

3   It increases

4   C

16.3

1   Your weight

2   a   Newtons (N)   b   Kilograms (kg)

3   B

4   Earth

16.4

1   D

2   Watt (W)

3   runner A

4   C

16.5

1   Elastic – returns to original shape or size.
    Inelastic – doesn't return to original shape or size.

2 a Extension = new length – original length

b Steel spring

c Steel spring

d It didn't return to its original length.

17.1

1 m/s

2 A

3 C

17.2

1 It increases

2 Increase

3 Increase

4 Any **one** from: speed of the car; friction between the road and tyres; the mass of the car; the condition of brakes and tyres.

17.3

1 a D   **b** A   **c** C   **d** B

   e 1 m/s   **f** 0.75 m/s

2 Scalar

17.4

1 Vector

2 m/s^2

3 B

4 D, A, C, E, B

17.5

1 a B–C   **b** A–B   **c** C–D

2 a BC   **c** CD

   b AB   **d** $1 m/s^2$

18.1

1 Clockwise ↺ from left: nucleus, electron, proton, neutron.

2 Alpha, beta, gamma

3 Radioactive decay

4 Photographic film, Geiger counter

18.2

1 a Gamma   **b** Alpha   **c** Beta

2 Alpha – about 5 cm – thin sheet of paper. Beta – about 1 m – 5 mm aluminium. Gamma – unlimited – thick sheet of lead or concrete.

3 Mutations or cancer

4 Alpha

5 Any **two** from: keeping their distance, using tools with long handles, keeping out of radioactive areas, using lead or concrete shielding, wearing a badge to measure how much radiation they are exposed to

18.3

1 B, A, D, C

2 Alpha radiation is absorbed by the plastic case.

3 a It will decrease / go down.

   b It will increase / go up.

4 a It is less ionising.

   b It would be absorbed by the tissues of the body.

18.4

1 Becquerels (Bq)

2 The activity to fall to half of its initial value.

3 2 minutes

4 Number of neutrons

18.5

1 Radioactive contamination – the presence of radioactive materials where they shouldn't be.

Half-life – the time it takes for the activity of a radioactive source to fall to half of its initial value.

Irradiation – the exposure of an object to ionising radiation.

2 A No   **B** Yes

   C Medical equipment and dressings

3 A greater risk than those with a short-half life (because they remain radioactive for longer).

Component 5: Exam-style questions

1 a Solar [1]

   b Renewable [1]

2 Sound energy transferred to the surroundings. [1]

3 a From top: true [1], false [1], false [1], true [1]
   b Electricity [1]
4 a Y [1]
   b Kinetic [1]; gravitational potential [1]
5 a Thinking distance - distance a car travels whilst the driver reacts; braking distance - Distance a car travels once the breaks have been applied [1]
   b Speed of car [1]
   c Rain [1]
   d Friction [1]
6 a $\dfrac{125\,m}{5\,s}$ [1] =25 m/s [1]
   b m/s [1]
   c Forwards acceleration arrow smaller than the backwards drag force arrow. [1 mark for labelled arrows, 1 mark for size of arrows]
7 a Between the paper and the aluminium. [1]
   b Medical tracer [1]
   c Any **one** from: is hard to stop [1] **or** can go through the body. [1]
8 a Labelled thermometer. [1]
   b 5 minutes [1]
   c Bar drawn up to the 4 minutes. [1]
   d Cotton wool [1]

Component 5: Exam-style questions (Trilogy)

01.1 Non-renewable [1]
01.2 It produces radioactive waste. [1]
02.1 12 [1]
02.2 6 [1]
02.3 Carbon 14 has 2 more neutrons than Carbon 12. [1]
02.4 Between 5500–6500 years [1]
03   Becquerel (Bq) [1]
04.1 Newtons [1]
04.2 Jupiter [1]
04.3 50 kg × 3.8 N/kg [1] = 190 N [1]
05.1 Work done = force × distance [1]
05.2 50 N × 15 metres [1] = 600 J [1]
06.1 speed = distance × time [1]
06.2 B-C [1]
06.3 3 km [1]
06.4 D-E [1]
06.5 The rate of change of velocity / speed. [1]
06.6 A-B [1], E-F [1]
07.1 Forward force arrow for acceleration [1]; backwards arrow for air resistance. [1]
07.2 Gravitational store [1]; kinetic [1]
08.1 105 − 50 = 55 [1]
08.2 Correctly plotted point at (3 N, 55 mm) [1]
09.1 $\dfrac{600}{800}$ × 100 [1] = 75 % [1]
09.2 Student A [1]. Energy can only be transferred, not destroyed. [1]

19.1

1 Current
2 a Ammeter – amps, Voltmeter – volts.
   b Current   c Voltage
3 a It will be off.
   b There will be no reading (no current).
4 Difficult OR hard, decrease OR reduce

19.2

1 Coulombs (C)
2 dc – charge keeps moving in the same direction; ac – charge constantly changes direction.
3 a A   b B
4 a ac   b 230 V   c dc

19.3

1 Ohms (Ω)
2 A
3 Increase

19.4

1 B, A, D, C, E
2 Filament lamp – lights up. Resistor – resists the flow of electric current. Diode – only allows the current to flow in one direction. Thermistor/LDR – resistance decreases as light or temperature increases.

3 X – filament lamp, Y – resistor, Z – diode

19.5

1 Series – Y, parallel – X

2 X

3 **a** Ammeter: 1   **b** Voltmeter: 2

4 True: B, C, D. False: A, E

20.1

1 Earth – green/yellow. Live – brown. Neutral – blue.

2 A – earth, B – neutral, C – fuse, D – live wire, E – cable grip

3 Blow OR melt (and the flow of electric current will stop).

20.2

1 **a** (metal) case and the earth

    b From the case to the earth.

    c Blow OR melt and the current will stop.

    d Into the user causing an electric shock.

2 There is an extra layer of insulation that stops the live wire touching the case.

3 3 A, 5 A, 13 A

4 **a** It would blow OR melt straight away.

    b It wouldn't blow OR wouldn't give you any protection.

20.3

1 Watts (W)

2 D

3 A, B, C

4 Kilowatt hours (kWh)

20.4

1 Transferred per second

2 A

3 D

20.5

1 Power station – these generate electricity. Step-up transformer – increases the potential difference. Step-down transformer – decreases the potential difference. Transmission cables – allow electrical current to flow.

2 C, E, B, A, D

3 smaller; reduces; increases

21.1

1 Non-contact

2 W – attract, X – repel, Y – repel, Z – attract

3 X – magnetic field around a bar magnet. Y – magnetic field when two like poles meet. Z – magnetic field when two opposite poles meet.

21.2

1 **a** It would increase

    b It would decrease

2 X – magnetic field pattern around a solenoid

    Y – magnetic field pattern around a wire

3 Electromagnet

21.3

1 **a** Pick up more   **b** Current

2 You can switch off the magnet to drop the cars.

3 D, A, C, B

21.4

1 The arrows point from the south pole to the north pole.

2 The plotting compasses in a line, needles pointing from N to S along the field line:

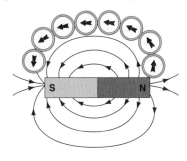

3 Induced

22.1

1 transverse, longitudinal

2 **a** up and down   **b** left to right

3 **a** left to right   **b** left to right

4 Compressions – where the spring is bunched up. Rarefactions – where the coils are spaced out.

22.2

1 Amplitude – maximum displacement. Frequency – number of waves per second. Wavelength – the distance point to point from one wave to the next. Peak – maximum upwards displacement. Trough – maximum downward displacement.

2 A – peak, B – trough, C – amplitude, D – wavelength, E – frequency

22.3

1 B

2 B, D, A, C, F, E

3 C

23.1

1 Transverse

2 Radio waves, microwaves, infrared, visible light, ultraviolet, x-rays, gamma rays

3 Ultraviolet, x-rays, gamma rays

23.2

1 Visible light – seeing with our eyes. Microwaves – cooking food. Radio waves – carrying TV signals. Infrared – heat lamps, TV remote controls.

2 Radio waves

3 Microwaves

4 Visible light

5 Infrared

23.3

1 Gamma rays – killing cancer cells, ultraviolet – sun lamps, x-rays – seeing inside the body

2 Ultraviolet

3 Kill them / damage them / damage the DNA / cause mutations

4 To sterilise them / kill the bacteria

23.4

1 kg/m³

2 B

3 C, A, D, B, E

23.5

1 Solid – Y – particles vibrate in fixed positions
   Liquid – Z – particles in contact with each other, move randomly
   Gas – X – particles much further apart, move randomly at faster speeds

2 Internal energy

3 it would increase

23.6

1 D, A, C, F/B, F/B, E

2 100 g (the same)

3 a A, D, B, C   b A and C

Component 6: Exam-style questions

1 a Complete [1]
   b True [1]; False [1]
   c Direct current [1]
   d 230 V [1]

2 9 A [1]

3 a The iron [1]
   b 0.03 kWh [1]

4 a The magnets repel. [1]
   b The magnets attract. [1]
   c Non-contact

5 Strength will increase. [1]

6 Ammeter [1]; voltage [1]; current [1]; resistance [1]

7 a False [1]; True [1]; False [1]; True [1]
   b They are dangerous / can cause cancer / damage cells. [1]

8 a Transverse – light wave; longitudinal – sound wave [1]
   b Arrow from left to right (horizontal). [1]
   c Arrow from centre to top of peak / bottom of trough. [1]

Component 6: Exam-style questions (Trilogy)

01.1 Resistance $= \dfrac{\text{potential difference (voltage)}}{\text{current}}$ [1]

01.2 $\dfrac{15}{5}$ [1] $= 3\,\Omega$ [1]

02.1 A [1]

02.2 C [1]

02.3 B [1] and C [1]

02.4 A series circuit has only one path. [1]
A parallel circuit has more than one path / has branches. [1]

02.5 A [1] . Because it has the highest total resistance (20 + 20 = 40). [1]

03.1 Power = $\dfrac{\text{energy transferred}}{\text{time}}$ [1]

03.2 Power = potential difference × current [1]

03.3 460 W [1]

04.1 Transformers increase or decrease the potential difference (voltage). [1]

04.2 Lower current can be used to transfer the same amount of energy. [1]
The wires will get less hot. [1]
Less energy is wasted as heat. [1]

05 Decreases [1]

06.1 Attracted [1]

06.2 Any **one** from: iron; cobalt; nickel; steel [1]

06.3 **One** from: car scrapyard, hospitals, induction hob [1]

07 Transverse wave transfers energy at right angles (perpendicular) to the direction of the oscillations. [1]
Longitudinal waves transfer energy parallel to the direction of the oscillations. [1]

08 400 [1] m/s [1]

09.1 Ice [1]

09.2 kg/m^3 [1]

09.3 1 kg of steam [1]

09.4 The particles in a solid vibrate in a fixed position. [1]
As the ice is warmed, the particles vibrate more / have more internal energy. [1]
The particles in a liquid are touching but can move about. [1]

Periodic table

Key	
relative atomic mass	
atomic symbol	
name	
atomic (proton) number	

Example:
1
H
hydrogen
1

1	2		3	4	5	6	7	0
								4 **He** helium 2
7 **Li** lithium 3	9 **Be** beryllium 4		11 **B** boron 5	12 **C** carbon 6	14 **N** nitrogen 7	16 **O** oxygen 8	19 **F** fluorine 9	20 **Ne** neon 10
23 **Na** sodium 11	24 **Mg** magnesium 12		27 **Al** aluminium 13	28 **Si** silicon 14	31 **P** phosphorus 15	32 **S** sulfur 16	35.5 **Cl** chlorine 17	40 **Ar** argon 18

39 **K** potassium 19	40 **Ca** calcium 20	45 **Sc** scandium 21	48 **Ti** titanium 22	51 **V** vanadium 23	52 **Cr** chromium 24	55 **Mn** manganese 25	56 **Fe** iron 26	59 **Co** cobalt 27	59 **Ni** nickel 28	63.5 **Cu** copper 29	65 **Zn** zinc 30	70 **Ga** gallium 31	73 **Ge** germanium 32	75 **As** arsenic 33	79 **Se** selenium 34	80 **Br** bromine 35	84 **Kr** krypton 36
85 **Rb** rubidium 37	88 **Sr** strontium 38	89 **Y** yttrium 39	91 **Zr** zirconium 40	93 **Nb** niobium 41	96 **Mo** molybdenum 42	[98] **Tc** technetium 43	101 **Ru** ruthenium 44	103 **Rh** rhodium 45	106 **Pd** palladium 46	108 **Ag** silver 47	112 **Cd** cadmium 48	115 **In** indium 49	119 **Sn** tin 50	122 **Sb** antimony 51	128 **Te** tellurium 52	127 **I** iodine 53	131 **Xe** xenon 54
133 **Cs** caesium 55	137 **Ba** barium 56	139 **La*** lanthanum 57	178 **Hf** hafnium 72	181 **Ta** tantalum 73	184 **W** tungsten 74	186 **Re** rhenium 75	190 **Os** osmium 76	192 **Ir** iridium 77	195 **Pt** platinum 78	197 **Au** gold 79	201 **Hg** mercury 80	204 **Tl** thallium 81	207 **Pb** lead 82	209 **Bi** bismuth 83	[209] **Po** polonium 84	[210] **At** astatine 85	[222] **Rn** radon 86
[223] **Fr** francium 87	[226] **Ra** radium 88	[227] **Ac*** actinium 89	[261] **Rf** rutherfordium 104	[262] **Db** dubnium 105	[266] **Sg** seaborgium 106	[264] **Bh** bohrium 107	[277] **Hs** hassium 108	[268] **Mt** meitnerium 109	[271] **Ds** darmstadtium 110	[272] **Rg** roentgenium 111	[285] **Cn** copernicium 112	[286] **Nh** nihonium 113	[289] **Fl** flerovium 114	[289] **Mc** moscovium 115	[293] **Lv** livermorium 116	[294] **Ts** tennessine 117	[294] **Og** oganesson 118

*The lanthanides (atomic numbers 58–71) and the actinides (atomic numbers 90–103) have been omitted.

Relative atomic masses for **Cu** and **Cl** have not been rounded to the nearest whole number.

Great Clarendon Street, Oxford, OX2 6DP, United Kingdom

Oxford University Press is a department of the University of Oxford.
It furthers the University's objective of excellence in research, scholarship,
and education by publishing worldwide. Oxford is a registered trade mark
of Oxford University Press in the UK and in certain other countries

British Library Cataloguing in Publication Data
Data available

ISBN 978-0-19-844498-5

10 9 8

Paper used in the production of this book is a natural, recyclable product
made from wood grown in sustainable forests.
The manufacturing process conforms to the environmental regulations
of the country of origin.

Printed in China by Shanghai Offset Printing Products Ltd

Acknowledgements
The publisher and authors would like to thank the following for
permission to use photographs and other copyright material:
Cover: Nattapong Tain/Shutterstock
p42, 56, 63: Shutterstock

Artwork by Aptara Inc. and Q2A Media Services Inc.

The authors would like to thank the editorial team at OUP for all of their
help and support on this project.

Every effort has been made to contact copyright holders of material
reproduced in this book. Any omissions will be rectified in subsequent
printings if notice is given to the publisher.